BUILDING PERFORMANCE-BASED
360 DEGREE
ASSESSMENTS:
FROM DESIGN TO DELIVERY

BY **LAWRENCE JOHN CIPOLLA** **cci surveys**
International

Building Performance-Based 360-Degree Assessments: From Design to Delivery

By Lawrence John Cipolla
President and Director, CCi Surveys International

For information, address inquiries to publisher.

This book may be purchased for educational, business, and sales promotional use.

ISBN 10: 1-59298-272-7
ISBN 13: 978-1-59298-272-1

Library of Congress Catalog Number: 2008944369

Book design and layout: Rick Korab, Punch Design, Inc.
Minneapolis, Minnesota, USA • punch-design.com

Research Writing Editor: Jennifer C. Manion
Minneapolis, Minnesota, USA • manionrwe.com

Proofreader: Michele B. Bassett
St. Paul, Minnesota, USA

Printed in the United States of America

First Printing 2009

13   12   11   10   09   5   4   3   2   1

Adams Business & Professional

7104 Ohms Lane, Suite 101
Edina, Minnesota 55439 USA
(952) 829-8818
www.BeaversPondPress.com

To order, visit www.BookHouseFulfillment.com or call
1-800-901-3480. Reseller and special sales discounts available.

Table of Contents

Table of Contents (continued)

P R E F A C E

Three-hundred and sixty-degree feedback has come a long way since I first used the concept in the early 1970s as a Spencer Foundation Research Fellow at the University of Minnesota. The results of my research and this comparative multi-perspective approach helped me earn my job as an external consultant at the 3M Company and three months later as a full-time employee.

Three-hundred and sixty-degree feedback has evolved from a stand-alone product to a process for development; from an alternative and supplement to identify an employee's strengths and areas for development to a path for helping people reach their potential; from an oddity (and perhaps a soon-to-pass fad) and something totally different to an integral part of an employee's development, both personal and professional.

Selling a 360-degree feedback assessment was a challenge in those early years of the 1970s. Few human resource people wanted to risk their reputations on this "new appraisal" process. Few understood the differences between style-type surveys and 360-degree feedback. Fewer still grasped the value of multiple raters versus boss-only feedback. Some managers saw the 360-degree process as a direct threat to their power and their role as sole source or primary source of performance appraisals. And, to some extent, these same apprehensions exist today.

In the mid-1980s I created a two-day on-site workshop that helped trainers and developers create more effective performance-based feedback assessments. That workshop is the foundation of this book. There are many articles and books on various aspects of 360-degree feedback. Yet, what was missing from my point of view was a guide and resource people could use to create their own assessments — assessments that focused on performance, what people do on the job. I believe you have that guide and resource in front of you now. I believe this also is the first book that discusses Web-based feedback.

HOW THIS BOOK IS ORGANIZED

The modular format of this book provides the reader with a structured and systematic approach to the design, development, and delivery of performance-based feedback. This book includes dozens of practical ideas and techniques the reader can apply immediately. There are diagrams, tables and matrices, application exercises, competency models, and questions to get you thinking about your next feedback project.

Module One: Perspectives. This module clarifies the differences between the two basic types of feedback and when to use each one. There is a brief overview to 360-degree feedback and its ever growing use and popularity, including why people use it and why they tend to fear it.

Module Two: Designing It. This module focuses on the design elements you need to consider when creating the framework for any 360-degree assessment. This module clarifies the differences between competencies and behaviors, knowledge, skills, and attitudes, and how to identify the critical competencies and behaviors to include in your assessment that apply to all employees or to a specific target population.

Module Three: Developing It. When you develop an assessment, you make your design come alive. This module focuses on how to write the actual questions, lead-in statements, rater response scales, importance ratings, free-text and demographic questions for your assessment. This module discusses the merits of single versus dual response scales; odd versus even response scales; gap analysis and the value of directional feedback for helping participants apply their feedback to the workplace.

Module Four: Deploying It. This module should provide you with practical suggestions for deploying your Web-based survey effectively; the value of randomizing your questions; the most common types of rater bias; and how to ensure initial success for your 360-degree feedback project.

Module Five: Delivering It. This module identifies different ways to present the feedback results to participants; the five types of feedback participants can expect to receive; and samples for presenting the feedback in one page to multi-page reporting formats.

Appendix. The Appendix includes a comparison of data collection methods (electronic versus paper) and identifies different agendas you can use in structured workshop settings to guide participants through their feedback results. The Appendix also includes a discussion of basic psychometrics and their application to 360-degree assessments and the value of norms and behavior change. There are summary checklists for ensuring long-term success and personal accountability. The Appendix concludes with practical suggestions for integrating the 360-degree feedback process with other organizational training and development programs and examples that illustrate how some participants have responded to their feedback.

ACKNOWLEDGEMENTS

I will be ever grateful for the experiences I had as a Spencer Foundation
Research Fellow and as an external consultant, soon to become employee,
of the 3M Company. What I learned during those five formative years
helped me start my own company and become identified as one of
the pioneers in the design, development, and delivery of
performance-based 360-degree feedback.

I owe a major debt of gratitude to my clients, especially in those early days,
who had the confidence and trust in me and my assessments and
who took the risk to bring a new idea and a new consultant into
their organization. They had the courage to apply my message.

I believe I also owe some thanks to those who rejected (me and) this kind
of feedback. Their rejection helped me make my process more relevant and
more effective. Their rejection reinforced my belief that 360-degree
feedback was not a product or one-off event, but an ongoing process,
a process that invited continuous improvement and served as a catalyst
for implementing needed behavioral change.

I want to thank my wife and buddy, Judy, who left her professional career
to help us build a successful company and who, over these many years,
has endured my "out-of-the-box-ideas" and challenged them with her
"now what?" questions and doubts. While some of those ideas failed,
many more succeeded and helped to identify our company as the
innovative leader in multi-rater feedback around the world.

I also want to thank you, the reader of my book, for your willingness to read
what I have to offer and, ideally, your willingness to apply what
you have learned to your next feedback project.

Building Performance-Based 360-Degree Assessments: From Design to Delivery

Why This Book Now

This book focuses on 360-degree feedback, specifically performance-based 360-degree feedback. Performance-based feedback focuses on what people do on the job. That is, it is about observable job-related behaviors and is directly correlated to a person's performance. This kind of assessment does not measure attitudes. It is not about what people prefer to do or would like to do. It is not about what they know, but how effectively they apply what they know. It is about the consequences of one's actions on the job. In essence, 360-degree performance-based assessment provides a person with feedback about his or her effectiveness in job-related roles and related tasks.

The objective of this book is to provide you with key insights and best practices to consider, whether you intend to create your own 360-degree assessments or intend to have someone do this for you, whether you are internal to your organization or external to it.

This comprehensive book provides external consultants, HR professionals, and developers of performance-based assessments with the practical tools and guidance they need to design, develop, deploy, and deliver results to individuals and key decision makers.

This book will give decision makers, project leaders, and managers of developers a proven, structured approach for initiating and delivering a 360-degree assessment program. Further, it provides proven techniques for enlisting the support and commitment of personnel who will be evaluated and asked to evaluate others using a 360-degree assessment. If followed, the suggestions here will ensure the overall long-term success of the 360-degree process.

This book will help any developer and decision maker identify which competencies and behaviors to measure and why. This guide will help them discover what to include in their 360-degree assessment in order to reinforce current performance expectations as well as identify future issues that could impact the competitive viability of the organization.

This book incorporates a structured approach with examples of best practices. It includes many proven techniques and recommendations for getting any 360-degree feedback project right the first time.

Labels and Terms

The terms "surveys," "instruments," and "assessments" and "assessment tools" are interchangeable for the purposes of this book, and I use the term "assessments" more than I do the other terms. Each of these words refers to a means of or a format for collecting information.

External consultants and internal practitioners do not use the terms "themes," "competencies," "skills," or "practices" consistently for either a 360-degree assessment or for any assessment-appraisal process. More often than not I will use "themes" and "competencies" interchangeably to identify general subject topics such as "communication," "problem solving," "decision making," "motivating others," "delegating," "integrity," and so on.

I use the terms "behaviors" and/or "practices" to identify the observable actions that comprise and measure a theme or competency. Behaviors and practices are the issues one wants to measure in a 360-degree assessment and I use "survey questions," "survey items," "behaviors," and "practices" interchangeably with respect to the topic of this book.

People use different terms when referring to the person they report to. The less profane terms include "boss," "manager," and "supervisor." I use the generic and universal term "boss" to mean any individual who has direct reports. The "boss" is in a managerial position and includes supervisors, middle managers, and upper-level executives. Someone who has a managerial title but no direct reports is not a boss.

I have minimized my usage of "him/her," "he/she," "they/them," "us/ours," and "his/hers." I use "(s)he" to refer to both men and women.

I use the word "participant" throughout this book to refer to the person who is being evaluated or assessed by others. "Raters" refer to those folks who provide feedback on and to the participant. Raters can be the boss, direct reports, co-workers, peers, colleagues, team members, and customers (internal or external). Participants are also raters, because they assess themselves. I use the term "raters" to mean anyone who provides feedback on an assessment and I use the term "rater groups" to mean a single rater or a collection of raters who fit a specific demographic, such as a peer rater group or a customer rater group. A single boss, while not a group, is considered a rater group. Likewise, the participant is a rater group.

The Author and CCi Surveys International

My motivation for writing this book was to identify the issues and actions people take that can determine the success or failure of a 360-degree feedback project, not to write a "feel-good" book about the process. I also did not want to write a book that focused on the negatives. I did want to write about what decision makers, participants, raters, HR personnel, and internal or external developers do to lay the foundations for success or failure. I wrote this book to share what I have learned since the early 70s.

Working with clients around the world, I have been designing and delivering 360-degree feedback to clients since 1976, and have worked with large and smaller organizations, from those with less than 15 employees to those with more than 400,000. I have also worked with employees at all levels, from CEOs and Managing Directors to middle managers, from supervisors and team leaders to individual contributors. On the whole, I have actively managed hundreds of successful 360-degree feedback interventions throughout the world with clients in business, industry, government, and education.

You may have read about 360-degree assessments from others. You may be using a 360-degree assessment instrument now. Perhaps you have written or plan to write your own instrument. I invite you to read this book and learn from it. You can agree or disagree with my suggestions; after all, these are my opinions. But I can assure you that all are client-proven. At the very least, I trust that these ideas will help you think through what you have done, what you are doing, and what you could be doing to create better feedback instruments and processes than the ones you use or are considering. If in your reading of this book you sense that I am passionate about the subject, you are correct. If you sense that I am critical of some 360-degree assessments, you are correct again.

I consider myself bilingual. I speak training and the language of 360-degree feedback.

I first learned about the concept and value of multi-rater feedback as a Spencer Foundation Research Fellow at the University of Minnesota (1971-1972). I learned more and refined what I needed to know as an employee with 3M Company (1972-1976).

I then started my company in 1976. And I absolutely love what I do for a living. As I've said, I have been fortunate to travel not only all over the United States but across the globe. On my travels, I have helped people understand how they can implement performance-based 360-degree assessments more effectively. I've witnessed many success stories as well as a few spectacular phenomenal and colossal failures. On balance, though, there have been many more successes than failures.

CCi Surveys International (formally dba CCi Assessment Group International) has been a pioneer in the 360-degree feedback movement. In fact, I designed and marketed our first assessment instrument, the Leadership Development Profile, in 1980, basing it on the general multi-rater feedback process used by 3M Company in the early 1970s. We used that process in our needs analyses to identify customer-driven needs for developing market specific sales training. We did not call it 360-degree feedback then, but by the mid '80s the term was used widely and easily recognized.

Our organization was the first to integrate 360-degree feedback with training and development, self-directed action planning, and pre and post follow-ups. The goals of our feedback process were to help participants understand the consequences of their behavior and help them reach their potential through action planning and personal accountability. The CCi Surveys International feedback process looks like this:

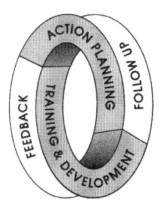

. . . . continuous learning for personal and professional development®

We market our performance-based assessments directly to our clients and through qualified CCi partners around the world. Our CCi partners include psychologists, OD and HR consultants, people at trade associations, and administrators at colleges and universities.

Dedication

I dedicate this book to my mother and father, who worked harder and longer than they needed to so their three children, my older brother, me, and my younger sister, could benefit from higher education and lead better lives. They were the first in our family, on both sides, to send all of their children to graduate school and on to very successful careers. Thank you Mom and Dad!

BUILDING PERFORMANCE-BASED

360 ASSESSMENTS: DEGREE

FROM DESIGN TO DELIVERY

A COMPREHENSIVE GUIDE
TO DESIGNING,
DEVELOPING, DEPLOYING,
AND DELIVERING
PERFORMANCE-BASED
360° FEEDBACK THROUGH
WEB-BASED SOFTWARE

BY **LAWRENCE JOHN CIPOLLA**

Module Focus

Clarifying the differences between micro and macro surveys; a background and historical perspective; identifying what is 360-degree feedback; why some people fear it; and why others embrace it; ensuring long-term success.

PERSPECTIVES

DESIGNING IT

DEVELOPING IT

DEPLOYING IT

DELIVERING IT

Micro and Macro Feedback

S urveys, questionnaires, opinion polls, entrance polls, exit polls, feedback tools, and other assessments are basically methods for collecting information from people about a wide range of topics, skills, issues, competencies, and themes. These tools help you document and organize what you want to learn about people or things from a defined target population.

There are basically two types of feedback: micro and macro. You can collect information on individuals or groups of people, on an individual thing or on a collection of things. Macro instruments collect information about a group, a team, a division, an organization, and things like products, services, and programs. Opinion, satisfaction, market research, and organizational climate surveys are examples of macro instruments. Micro instruments collect information on a single individual within a group or organization. 360-degree performance-based feedback is a micro assessment. Micro and macro assessments do not yield right or wrong answers. Rather, each poses a statement or question, aggregates the results, and identifies areas of strength and weakness, of satisfaction and dissatisfaction, of agreement and disagreement, and so on.

There is some confusion about what is or is not a 360-degree assessment instrument. You can make the argument that a macro instrument is a type of 360-degree instrument. With macro instruments you collect feedback on a theme from multiple internal and/or external sources and then compile the results according to different departments and functions; different positions and roles; different kinds of employees, such as exempt and non-exempt employees, full- and part-time employees; different locations, customers, and clients; and a wide range of other demographics relevant to the organization. However, macro instruments focus on overall areas of satisfaction or agreement or effectiveness or trends about a group *but not on the effectiveness of any one person.* That is the role of a micro instrument.

The difference between micro and macro feedback is not unlike the difference between the words "knight" and "night." They sound the same, but serve totally different purposes.

Neither the different sources of feedback nor multiple rater groups you use to collect feedback determine the difference between a micro and a macro instrument. When the instrument's target population or focal point is a single individual, it is a micro instrument. Performance-based 360-degree feedback focuses on what a single person does on the job. Performance-based feedback focuses on one person's effectiveness or level of satisfaction others have with one person's behaviors or actions. When you want to assess a specific individual, when you want to identify the specific strengths and developmental needs of a named individual, you are referring to and need a micro instrument. When you want to collect information from multiple sources on a specific individual you are generally referring to a 360-degree or a multi-rater process.

A few years ago, we had a client who was apprehensive about conducting a 360-degree customer satisfaction survey, and so initially he wanted a customer satisfaction survey (a macro instrument). The 360-degree survey would assess the effectiveness of individual salespeople, and the primary objections to this method came from the national sales manager who felt that customers might say things that would be detrimental to him. If customers identified weaknesses in his sales force, wouldn't that mean that he was not doing his job effectively? Yet, if he took action on their feedback and changed the way he had been doing things, wouldn't that mean that what he had been doing was wrong? And if he had been wrong, how would that affect his position (i.e., his job security)?

Sometimes personal agendas stand in the way of change. Sometimes egos stymie progress. Assessment tools do not cause people to have those opinions. They document what people are thinking. Once you have the data, positive and negative, you can take a proactive approach to build upon your successes and resolve your weaknesses. The project was implemented effectively. The national sales manager was touted as progressive for taking the initiative on the project. Smiles were had by all. Life went on.

Macro Feedback:
Employee Opinion, Organizational Climate,
Training Needs Analysis, Customer Satisfaction

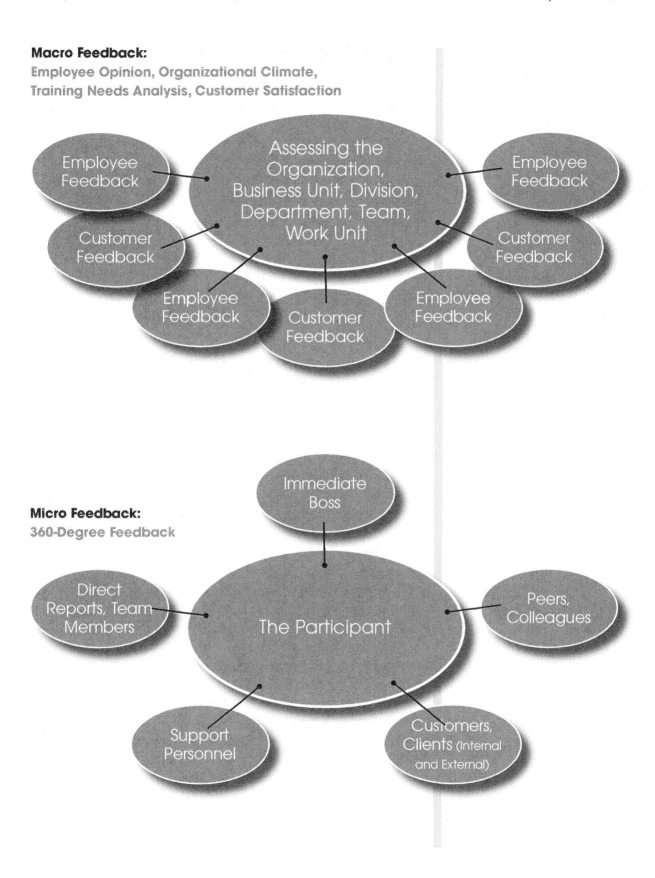

Micro Feedback:
360-Degree Feedback

Which Comes First?

Should you begin your evaluation of your organization with a macro instrument or a micro instrument? To know, you need to answer some questions. What do you want to learn? What is your goal and purpose? Do you want to learn about the organization in general? Do you want to look at group, functional, or organizational issues first, then individual performance later? Or do you want to begin with individual performance, then expand outward to measure organizational themes and issues? Do you want to migrate from general to specific (macro to micro) or specific to general (micro to macro)? Do you prefer to play it safe? Are your employees receptive to giving and receiving feedback?

Macro feedback serves a purpose. For example, it can help identify levels of employee satisfaction regarding the benefits you provide. It can identify the trust employees have in the organization. It can identify their attitudes towards quality, customer service, and so on. It can identify how they perceive the effectiveness of those who run the show. Knowing all of this is great. However, once the data is analyzed the issue of accountability often goes unaddressed. That accountability rests solely with what upper management chooses to do with the information. The issue then becomes:

- *To what extent will upper management share the results?*
- *How much of that information is shared and with whom?*
- *What incentive does upper management have to share the results with anyone?*
- *What changes will management make as a result of the data?*
- *What if the changes fail or are met with skepticism?*
- *What if nothing is done with the data at all?*

Once upper management shares the data collected from the macro instrument, it is unlikely that specific employees will stand up and claim responsibility for any identified problems. Who will say, *Yes, I confess. I am the rascal who is not as effective in that area. That is why the quality of work in our department is low.* Who will stand up? The answer is no one. In essence, macro surveys can seem safer. They are not directed at any one person. When folks review macro data

As the individual becomes more effective, so does the organization. Organizational development begins with individual development.

we often hear them say, *We need to do a better job communicating more.* We almost never hear them say, *I need to do a better job communicating to specific people, or that specific department, etc.* A 360-degree assessment can identify those who need to say this, and can help people learn what they need to communicate and to whom.

Macro surveys can also seem easy. It is easy for the less competent, less motivated, less confident, and less committed folks to hide behind macro data. No one person takes personal responsibility for any weaknesses or areas of lowest satisfaction within the organization. Personal accountability is easier with a 360-degree assessment. However, unless you require and reinforce that accountability, not much will change with your 360-degree process either.

Sure, micro surveys can make folks less comfy. With micro feedback, it is more difficult for individuals to avoid feedback. There is nowhere to hide. The feedback is directed at a particular person. The raters selected provided that person with their feedback. It is not about an amorphic group, but about that person. If the participant chooses to ignore the feedback, that is his or her decision alone. Every person is responsible for the consequences of her or his actions. As a result, change must begin at the individual level. Organizations do not change on their own. The people within the organization need to effect change first. They need to affect how they get things done. The organization or group or the team changes as a result of what individuals do.

Performance Is Behavior Is Performance

You are what you do.

A person's behavior affects his or her performance. That is, performance equals behavior. You cannot separate an individual's performance from her or his behavior. Past behavior may not be a guaranteed predictor of future behavior, but it is often the best precursor or predictor of future behavior.

To help people change their behavior and improve their performance, you can parade folks through a battery of psychometric tests. You can send them to charm school. You can send them away for weeks at a time to expensive leadership development programs. Some folks return and apply what they have learned and some won't be willing to. Some even become more effective as a result and some will choose not to change. And, of course, some other folks could be gaming you from the beginning. That is, they know how to act during the exercises and while they are being observed, and they tend to say all the right things and know how to play specific roles. They know how to take tests and how to say and do the right things. Some are adept at fooling observers, facilitators, and their fellow role-playing partners. These folks probably won't change even if given the chance.

Ultimately, what people do on the job, day in and day out, is critical for the organization. It is that performance, that behavior, which separates knowledge awareness from knowledge application. Performance-based 360-degree assessments can identify those behaviors that are effective and perhaps not as effective for participants. They can help participants understand the consequences of their actions.

Origin of the Species

A circle, with its 360 degrees, is a mathematical concept. The folks who invented the wheel, the Mesopotamians (about 5000-6000 years ago), may have had some influence in developing the concept, as may have the Babylonians and then the Egyptians, who divided representations of the wheel, or circle, into 360 degrees. Archimedes and Claudius Ptolemy are famously associated with the concept.

The concept of 360 degrees applied to feedback is a somewhat newer concept, however. Different groups and people claim to be the father (or mother) of the concept. If the people at NASA can be called the progenitors, then so be it. NASA can be said to have created the concept in the 1960s to evaluate personnel integral to its space program. It was advertised as an efficient process for gathering objective evaluations about observed job-related behaviors.

The concept gained popularity through organizational usage and success stories. The explosive use came about in the late 1980s when a myriad of consultants decided to develop and use this method. And they did. The fact that several Fortune 1000 companies had class-action suits filed against them for biased performance appraisals helped to push the 360-degree process to a more center-stage role and may have motivated some consultants to jump on and ride the wave. And they did.

The accelerated rise in the use of multi-rater feedback is a direct result of the failure of traditional performance appraisal processes to actually appraise performance. The 1980s bore witness to shocking tales of managers who biased their appraisals. Words like "favoritism" and "cronyism" and "discrimination" were hurled about willy-nilly. Suddenly, organizations needed an alternative, an alternative that would counterbalance the traditional appraisal process. And so an industry was born. Actually two industries were born: a legal one of lawyers who represented class-action suits, and another of consultants who suddenly discovered the 360-degree concept. And then along came authors and gurus who saw linking a 360-degree process to their books or training programs as a really good thing. But that was in the old days. Nonetheless, the concept of 360-degree feedback has grown exponentially since the mid-80s and continues to grow to this day, despite its critics. At last unofficial count there are at least 300 vendors marketing some sort of 360-degree assessment product in the USA alone.

Many performance appraisals do not appraise performance.

What Is 360-Degree Feedback?

360-degree feedback goes by a number of stripes depending on the creativity of the vendor. It is marketed as multi-rater feedback, multi-source assessment, multi-point feedback, multi-source feedback, group performance review, 360-degree feedback, 360-degree assessment, 360-degree evaluation, full-circle feedback, full-circle appraisal, and plain old 360. When you include pre- and post-assessments, the labels "720-degrees" and "1440-degrees" reflect the number of assessments you can implement (i.e., 360 degrees x 2 or 360 degrees x 4). Marketing and vendor labeling aside, 360-degree feedback means that an individual receives feedback from multiple sources. Those sources may be internal or external to the organization. Typically, those sources are above, below, and at the same hierarchical level as the individual being assessed. In short, the individual (who we'll call the participant) is surrounded by feedback. A circle is a self-contained unit or system. There are 360 degrees in a circle. 360-degree or multi-rater feedback comes from people who know the participant very well. 360-degree feedback comes from people who are a part of the participant's circle or work unit system.

360-Degree Feedback:
Multiple Sources on a
Specific Participant

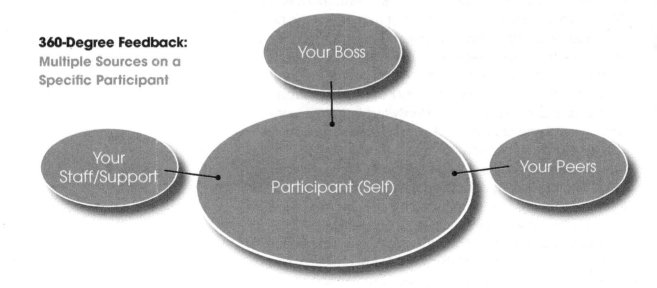

Why Use It

Performance-based 360-degree feedback is a tool that can identify how a person interacts with others. It can identify the effectiveness of a person's behavior vis-à-vis others. It can identify the consequences of a person's behavior on others. It can identify a person's strengths and weaknesses. It can identify hidden strengths. It can identify blind spots that could derail a career—even yours! 360-degree feedback is not about giving a score. It is about assessing a person's behavior and performance. Scores are handy when you want to rank people. Behavioral feedback is better when you want to help and have people change their behavior.

People act differently depending on whom they are with and the situation in which they happen to be. The collection of feedback from multiple sources assumes that each of these sources will have a different perspective of the participant and, therefore, offer the participant unique insights regarding how his or her behavior affects them. Credible and relevant feedback can help a person recognize those areas of performance that need improvement. It can help a participant understand what strengths to build upon for continued success and effectiveness. When one understands one's strengths and weaknesses, one can build upon those strengths and make needed changes in one's work behavior.

People often do not make changes because others want them to. People make changes when they see a need to do so. People make changes for their reasons, not those of others. They change their behavior when they understand their feedback and value that feedback from the people who provided it. They change their behavior when they understand the consequences for doing things differently. You can help them buy into their results by presenting the feedback in terms of:

- *Strengths* to build upon
- *Hidden strengths* to build upon
- *Developmental needs* for self-directed action planning
- *Discrepancies* to identify blind spots and potential barriers
  to career planning

Performance-based feedback acts as a catalyst for implementing needed change.

Performance-based 360-degree feedback can help unfreeze ineffective behavior. Use it as a pre- and post-application. Feedback provides a direction for initial change. It can provide baseline data for the participant to consider. Training, development, coaching, and other initiatives can follow as a result of the feedback. Your training and development initiatives thus become feedback (needs) driven. The second or post-feedback process can identify the effects of the participant's change efforts and what has yet to be developed. It can quantify (measure) progress.

What happens at the top cascades throughout the organization.

Why People Fear It

Some people fear it (a lot!). The shift of evaluation and assessment duties from an immediate supervisor to other rater groups has had interesting implications for both individuals and organizations. For example, raters want to know the extent to which their responses will be kept confidential and anonymous and how can they be assured of this. Participants want to know what will happen if the feedback identifies weaknesses. Will the results affect their performance appraisals, compensation, or chances for advancement? While different people have different fears, the concept of a 360-degree assessment is blameless. The primary reason for the fear factor is the way folks have corrupted its use and application, especially during its early development.

Bosses often fear they will lose (or have lost) their authority over their direct reports by allowing others to participate in the evaluation-assessment process. Some bosses cherish the need to control others. Apparently this goes with the title — the boss's. Not all bosses dislike 360-degree assessment of course. Yet many fear it because they do not like a process that isolates the boss's responses as a distinct line of feedback. Bosses may prefer to have their responses buried (hidden? merged? disguised?) in a rater group called "Others." Some may fondly recall how their favorite bosses had recalled single, not so-productive events, and used it in their performance appraisals. Some bosses fear there may be discrepancies between what they said on a performance appraisal and how they responded to the questions on the

360-degree assessment. Credibility may also be an issue. Consistency may be another issue. Finally, some bosses do not like the conflict that can arise when they have to tell the employees their performance does not meet expectations, no matter what kind of evaluation reveals the need to do so.

Direct reports often do not like the process, especially if their responses will be identified to the participant. Not all direct reports dislike 360-degree assessments. Yet they need to be certain their responses will remain confidential and anonymous. Some direct reports may have had experience with one of *those liberal-free-thinking-empowerment-to-all-diversity-embracing-I-love-everybody-just-ask-me-one-of-the-boys-one-of-the-girls bosses* who then made life miserable because the boss received feedback that was less than complimentary and attributed that feedback to a specific direct report. Most direct reports do not mind giving feedback. They often do mind being identified and being criticized and being ridiculed as the direct report who has an issue with another's behavior. They do mind being punished for providing open and honest feedback, only to then have the rug pulled out from under them.

Peers often do not like the process either. Of course, not all peers dislike the process, yet many fear it if they believe their responses will be identified. They may also fear that they will be selected as the next group to be evaluated. Some see the process as just another fad from human resources. Some take umbrage when they are evaluated by their colleagues even though most peer data, on average, is nicer than that provided by bosses or direct reports.

Team members do not like the process. Not all team members dislike it, of course, but some fear it because it could identify them as the weak link on the team. Other team members may know this already, but having it documented for all to see is a tad difficult to handle. As a result, team assessments that look at *Us* and *We* (macro) are easier to handle than a team assessment that looks at *You*. Team assessments that frame the questions from a *We* perspective rather than a *You* (micro) perspective are nicer, and, for that reason, are more popular (safer). A 360-degree team assessment that focuses on individual behavior can be uncomfortable to some folks.

If 360-degree feedback is so popular, why doesn't anyone use it?

Customers do not like 360-degree feedback. Well, not all customers dislike participating in the process, yet some fear it if they see giving such feedback as a way to trap them into buying more products and services, or of having someone find out what they *really* think of an organization! Some are concerned about their relationship with their salesperson. They may fear that giving negative comments will hurt the salesperson. Some are simply indifferent because they do not trust the intent of the process. That is, they do not trust how an organization will use their feedback, especially if they've felt ineffectual when giving similar feedback in the past.

Participants often really do not like the process. Well, not all participants dislike the process, but some less-than-mediocre employees do not want to know that *others* find their performance wanting. Other people just do not like to receive feedback. Some find it easier to give feedback and to criticize, rather than receive feedback and then have to do something positive with the results. Some will mistrust the entire process and at times their skepticism is warranted. But sometimes it is good old paranoia kicking in. Some do not want to be held accountable for their behaviors. Some participants see the need to satisfy their favorite bosses and so they tolerate their feedback. Upward feedback from underlings . . . well, that just seems to be so much bother. Some people believe that any form of appraisal is unnecessary. This may have something to do with entitlement and the rights of the individual. Some people believe they have a right to their particular job. Some people believe employees have the right to perform as they choose. Performance appraisals, 360-degree feedback, and feedback in general are thus viewed as infringements on the individual. The evaluation process smacks of big brother-ism. And there are some who believe raters will "gang up" on them and provide more negative feedback than is warranted.

So that is why some folks fear it. Performance-based 360-degree feedback is not woo-woo or touchy-feely stuff. It is not simply PC. It is not for sissies. Well designed 360-degree assessments can identify strengths and weaknesses. The strength part is easier to handle than the weakness part, and it is often the ability to pinpoint weaknesses that causes folks to run for the shadows. Self-only surveys and style-preference surveys can seem vanilla in comparison. According to the creators, there are no bad or weak styles; my preferences are no better than your preferences. With self-only surveys it is easy to gloss over your weaknesses, but there is nowhere to hide with 360-degree feedback. 360-degree feedback measures one person standing in front of a mirror, naked and exposed. One can assess oneself however one chooses. Comparing one's own assessment with those from twelve, fifteen, or thirty-five other raters is another matter. Of course, what a participant says is important. What other raters and rater groups say about a participant's performance is more important. What they uncover about that person's behavior may be frightening to him/her and cause palms to become moist. Yet for the vast majority of others, it is the opportunity to learn and apply the results in a positive and meaningful way.

360 can benefit any employee. It can benefit excellent as well as poor and mediocre performers. Unfortunately, the latter are less likely to want to be evaluated. They are not too keen about acknowledging their performance deficiencies and they are less likely to implement self-directed action plans than are the better performers.

360-degree feedback is for developing, not criticizing, the participant.

Why People Like It

So if people fear it so much, why even bother with it? The primary purpose of 360-degree feedback is developmental. It can help a person understand how different groups perceive his or her performance. It serves to balance the feedback received from a single source, such as a favorite boss. It allows one to compare one's relative effectiveness from any internal or external source. A well designed 360-degree assessment can help people understand the consequences of their behavior. It can identify strengths to build upon. It can identify weaknesses and areas to develop. It can identify potential career blocks. It can help people reach their potential! People like the balanced, multi-level feedback. They like it when they see that one rater group says they are highly effective on a particular behavior or practice. When other raters say the same thing, they can become euphoric, even giddy. It is one thing for the boss to say you are terrific;

Feedback is the

soul of champions.

to receive that same feedback from lots of other raters and rater groups is even better. There is a certain quality when numbers of raters provide one with positive feedback.

Highly motivated and effective people thrive on feedback. They want to become even more effective. Highly motivated participants find the substance for initiating needed change in their feedback. Their action plans have relevance not just for themselves but also for those with whom they interact. Effective people are proactive. They want to reach their potential. They want to excel. They understand that feedback can help them reach their goals. They understand that feedback is not criticism.

Proactive folks often prefer feedback systems that allow them to create sub-groups for gathering even more specific feedback. Salespeople, for example, can create multiple customer-client rater groups according to what customers purchase, how much they purchase, or how large or small the customer-client account is and so on. There are separate data lines for each customer sub-group. This more focused feedback acts as an individual market-research tool for that salesperson, who then can respond more proactively to the specific customer-types in her or his territory. The salesperson might think, *Here is what I need to do differently with this customer group (or all customer groups). Here is what I can build upon with that customer group (or all customer groups).*

Generally, participants like the 360-degree assessment process because they receive:

- *A clearer understanding of their strengths and developmental needs*
- *Comparative data on their effectiveness with those with whom they interact on a regular basis*
- *A structured, non-threatening way to discuss their strengths and weaknesses*
- *Developmental feedback, rather than criticism*
- *Directional feedback identifying what they can do more or less of to become even more effective*
- *A process for establishing better dialogues with their favorite bosses*
- *A process for establishing better dialogues with their direct reports, team members, peers, and customers*
- *A channel to review and discuss specific results with others*

- *Quantifiable and qualitative data to drive their self-directed action planning efforts*
- *A better understanding of the consequences of their behavior and how their behavior affects others*
- *Information that puts them in control of their personal and professional development*

How to Reduce the Fears

There will always be some people who distrust any feedback process. There will always be some people who do not believe that the survey design will yield what it promises. They may not trust how the organization will use or abuse feedback about them. If, as the result of the feedback, people are criticized, punished, ridiculed, or otherwise dealt with in a less than productive way, they will not trust the process. Fear develops. The 360 process did not cause the fear. The way the results were used did!

All projects have barriers. The difference between success and failure means recognizing and removing as many barriers as possible. Consider the following:

- **First, identify and eliminate as many barriers as possible.** *What could block the success of your feedback project? Use "force field analysis" or a "t-analysis" to identify what could stand in the way of success. Identify what will contribute to its success. How will you remove any barriers? How can you ensure success? Then make your go/no-go decision.*
- **Be aware of horror stories.** *What major disasters have you heard about? How can you prevent them from happening to you? Do you know organizations that have tried the process and failed in their efforts? If so, what happened? Why did it fail? Will your efforts realize the same end? What are you doing to make certain you do not become part of one of the horror stories yourself?*
- **Be clear about the purpose.** *Why are you doing this and who knows what you are thinking? Is the feedback for self-awareness? Self-development? Will it be used as part of the performance appraisal process? Will it replace the performance appraisal process? Will it be used to determine compensation? Do participants know how the results will be used? How will you communicate the purpose of the 360 process?*
- **Provide a channel of communication.** *Who can people contact with their questions and concerns about the process?*

- **Take your time.** *Why are you doing this now? Conduct a pilot session or two. What worked? What didn't? Resolve any potential problems before you unleash the full process and administer it within a business unit or throughout the organization.*
- **Be up-front about the results.** *Who owns the data after it is collected? Who will see the results and when? What will you say to a boss who wants a copy of someone's feedback? How will you handle confidentiality?*

That said, first and foremost (once again and again), the process should not be used to punish or criticize the participant. It should be used to develop the person. The process should help participants reach their potential. It should help them perform more effectively for their benefit and that of the department or organization.

Select feedback instruments that evaluate behaviors. The items on the survey should be observable and measurable. They could compare what the person is currently doing with what the expectations are for that person, according to each rater group.

Encourage participants to be more proactive in their own development, personal and professional. Employees should not wait for someone to take them by the hand. They cannot wait for things to fall into their laps. Encourage employees to go to others for advice and counsel and to initiate the process themselves. Encouraging them to share their feedback with others helps people understand that the process is for development, for becoming more effective.

Conduct structured sessions, either one-on-one or in a workshop, that include trained facilitators to help participants understand their feedback. Facilitators are guides. They guide participants through the interpretation of their data. They can help them create self-directed action plans. They can respond to their questions. They can act as temporary coaches. In short, they can help participants understand the consequences of their data, that no person is perfect, that having developmental needs is not the issue. Trained facilitators can help participants identify the real issues and move forward, identifying what they intend to do differently as a result of the feedback.

If you intend to measure participants' problem-solving and decision-making acumen, you should have a problem-solving and decision-making training program in place so participants can learn how to become more effective in that area. What about the other competencies in your 360 assessment? Does your organization have resources that people can access, internally or externally? If training is not an issue, do you have a coaching and mentoring program in place? Before you measure something, make certain you have developmental options available to participants who may need support once they receive their results. If they are not now available, when do you plan to have them?

What role will the immediate managers play after you assess participants? Will they act as positive role models? Will they act as willing coaches and provide ongoing feedback to reinforce participants' efforts to change? Do managers know how to provide constructive feedback? Will they be willing (required?) to be assessed as well?

You can reduce fears when you establish the 360 assessment as an ongoing process. Treat it as a one-off event and employees will view it as a borderline fad. The process will then suffer, along with your reputation.

360-degree feedback is an ongoing developmental process. It is not a single event.

Notes:

Module Focus

Identifying the basic design elements and options; creating competency models; deciding whose competencies to use; benchmarking; identifying and defining your core competencies.

PERSPECTIVES

DESIGNING IT

DEVELOPING IT

DEPLOYING IT

DELIVERING IT

Designing Your 360-Degree Assessment

Designing is not developing. People tend to confuse the two. You or an architect designs your home with a blueprint, a model, or a wish list of gotta-haves written on a napkin. You develop your home when someone constructs it from your wish list. The same applies to any feedback instrument. There are people who have an aptitude for designing instruments. They can outline the instrument's structure. They can talk conceptually. They can provide the big picture. They can outline the shape and scope of the instrument. Such folks effectively create the skeleton, the general form, and the framework of the instrument. All of this is important when you plan and design any assessment. Yet some folks talk about their design as though it were a complete ready-to-use assessment. It is not.

Even with the design in place, someone still has to write the actual instructions, and definitions, and items. Someone has to put the flesh on the skeleton and make the outline come alive. That is the development process, and building an instrument can take longer than you might think. It may cost you more than you budgeted. Furthermore, when you design and develop your instrument, you need to think about how you will collect and compile the data and produce the results. What you design and can deliver will be a function of the software features. You cannot include demographic items if your software has not been programmed to compile and report that type of information. What you design drives what you can develop. What you develop drives whether your instrument will be viewed as effective and a success or irrelevant and a waste of time and money. Designs are concepts. Development is the transformation of those ideas into a ready-to-use survey.

Your conceptual design can be simple or comprehensive. Either way, it should include some basic elements.

Designing an assessment is not the same as developing it.

Basic Design Elements

- *Title:* What will you call it?
- *Format:* How will you collect the feedback, on paper or electronically?
- *Description:* Who is the target population, e.g., a specific level of management, a particular division or business unit? What is the purpose of the assessment, e.g., for development, for complementing your in-house leadership or team-building program? When will participants see their data? Who else will see their data? What will participants be expected to do with their feedback?
- *Dimension:* Think of Dimensions as general headings. They include a set of related topics or competencies-themes for each heading. Dimensions are not usually defined.
- *Competency:* Listed below Dimensions are the competencies that are critical to your organization. Each competency has a logical link to each dimension. Competencies should be defined if you decide to include an "importance ratings" section in your instrument. Your definitions will prevent raters from defining a competency from their own perspectives. Definitions keep themes-competencies consistent by using a common language set.
- *Behaviors-Practices:* Listed beneath each competency are the observable behaviors and practices that are critical to the effectiveness of your employees. The behaviors and practices measure each competency based on your definition of that competency (or theme). You write these behaviors and practices in question format. Raters respond to these questions as they assess the participant. Consider at least five items per competency.

Optional Basic Design Elements

- *Demographic Items:* These items can make cross-correlations easy. Only participants respond to these items in a 360-degree instrument. Demographic items can identify who the participant is with respect to their gender, title, position, location, function, role, and number of years employed. You can compare one function with another or all other functions. You can compare locations and the effectiveness of one management level with another, and so on.
- *Importance Ratings:* These ratings can help you identify differences in priorities certain competencies-themes have between and among different rater groups. Importance ratings can identify deltas or gaps between what upper-level folks think is important and what the lower-level folks think is important. Sometimes what one group believes is important is not identified with what another group thinks.

- **Open-Ended:** *These are qualitative items. They can ask raters to expand on the feedback from the quantitative response scales. These items can elicit feedback about other areas. They can provide additional insights to participants.*

Getting Started

Your style of thinking and writing may be different than mine. I collaborate with my clients. I need some basic information about the target population, the purpose of the survey, why they have chosen to implement a 360-degree process now, and so on. As I think about the target population, the goals, and the purpose, I begin with the competencies that should meet the clients' expectations and the needs of the target population. You may do this differently. As a starting point, think about competencies you want to measure and why. Use a napkin. Do you think communication, delegating, team building, and personal integrity are relevant? You may prefer a more structured approach, such as outlining what you want to measure based on chats with other folks from your focus group sessions, and/or on information from your training needs analysis survey. You may talk about competency models. These models-topics-themes-subjects are your competencies.

What do you want to measure and why?

Competencies Defined

Clarify your terms. There is no consistent use of the word "competency" in 360 assessments. Some people interchange the word "competency" with "skill." Others use the term "practices." Some use the generic term "theme" to encompass a range of labels, excluding the actual questions on the assessment. Even the term "questions" is used inconsistently. What some vendors call "questions" when they design and implement assessment tools to measure competencies are sometimes called "items" or "behaviors" or "practices" by others. Yet others consider these "questions-items" to be "competencies" or "practices" or "skills." You will read about "core competencies," "essential competencies," "best practice competencies," "roles," and other terms depending on the creativity of the vendor and the latest buzz words. Labels are labels. Labels are irrelevant as long as everyone knows what the label means and what it refers to without ambiguity.

Be consistent in your use of a term or label. If you choose to refer to something as "Communicating with Others" and call it a competency (or theme or skill or subject or topic or practice or whiz-bang-woo-woo), then be consistent when you talk about it with others. If you choose to refer to "Consistently Completes Work On Time" as a competency (rather than as a behavior or practice or whatchamacallit), be consistent. You will need to clarify what you mean with the person who is developing your instrument for you. If you are that person and do not need to develop these labels with others, use them as you see fit. Whenever you are working with another person, internal or external, make certain all of you know what you are referring to and what each label means. If not, you will find yourself spinning your wheels and wondering *why the other person doesn't get it!* Remember: What is obvious to you may not be obvious to someone else. Again, clarify your labels up front.

Think Wittgenstein: If you define "red" as meaning "black," you have created a definition for "red." This now is the definition for red in your assessment. Raters may not agree with your definition but that is a moot point once you define it for the context of the assessment (or the context of anything else). Your definition excludes all others. Your definition channels the raters' thinking.

That said, what the heck is a competency?

Competency-Competence-Competent

Folks interchange and refer to these terms as though they are one and the same. They are not.

When used as nouns: "Competency" and "competence." When we refer to these terms we can discuss what it means to have competence: being in possession of required skills, knowledge, qualification, or capacity. Having competence is having the ability to perform activities to the standards required for employment, for example. Competence is a standard or stated skill level drawing upon an appropriate mix of knowledge and skills (i.e., abilities) required to do a specific task to a given level. Does the person have the competence to do this task this way or for this outcome? Some aspects of competency are:

- *The ability to know requirements necessary to perform an individual task*
- *The ability to manage or perform multiple tasks*
- *The ability to respond to unforeseen barriers or breakdowns*
- *The ability to work with others to get things done*

When used as adjectives: "Competent." When we say that someone is a competent employee, we can mean that the person has suitable or sufficient skills, knowledge, and experience for some purpose. The competent person is properly qualified given his or her knowledge, training, and experience. Competent people are competent not just for what they know, but for what they do and how they actually perform. Their performance is adequate. That is, it is acceptable, but it is not outstanding or exceptional. Did the person perform the task in a competent manner (based on some performance criteria)?

When applied to 360 assessments: "Competencies" is the general term for a knowledge set and set of applied skills a person must possess in order to perform a task successfully. Competencies are the combination of knowledge and skills that comprise that theme or competency. Competencies can be improved through practice and application. You can become more competent. Competencies can be learned.

Highly competent performers make demands on themselves. Less competent performers make demands on others.

People can be more or less competent when it comes to communicating, for example. You can think about communication as a:

- **Competency** – *a collection of knowledge and skills*
- **Skill** – *the ability and proficiency level when one communicates*
- **Attitude** – *the tone and style and manner, verbal and non-verbal, by or with which one communicates*
- **Behavior** – *the observable act or process of communicating by writing, by speaking, or by displaying gestures non-verbally; the act of communicating*

Dimensions

Some folks add another layer to their competency model. They include something called a dimension. This is a common practice and sometimes it clarifies things, while at other times it does not. Dimensions frame or identify a like set of competencies, competencies that are common to that dimension. Communication, for example, can be a dimension or macro label within your model. As a dimension, labels for the competencies identified could include "Presentation Skills," "Writing Skills," "Listening Skills," and "Non-Verbal Skills." Another dimension could be "Self-Management." Under this dimension you may have included competencies labeled "Confidence," "Adaptability," "Self-Starter," or "Personal Initiative." Some folks include their mission and values within their assessments. Some include something called their leadership essentials or core values. You can use these essentials or values as your dimension labels. For example:

Core Value Dimension: People with Passion
- *Competency: Building Relationships*
- *Competency: Managing Diversity*
- *Competency: Adaptability*
- *Competency: Influence-Persuasion*

Core Value Leadership Essential Dimension: Personal Integrity
- *Competency: Ethical Leadership*
- *Competency: Personal Accountability*

Core Value Dimension: Personal Skills

- *Competency: Empathy*
- *Competency: Motivation*
- *Competency: Self-Awareness*
- *Competency: Self-Regulation*
- *Competency: Social Skills*

Core Value Dimension: Management Skills

- *Competency: Developing Others*
- *Competency: Project Management*
- *Competency: Team Building*

Core Value Dimension: Lead the Business Forward

- *Competency: Demonstrate Business Knowledge*
- *Competency: Customer Focus*

Some developers add a macro header on top of the dimension header. This can be overkill. For example:

Macro Header: Sense of Urgency
Core Value Dimension: Performance Leadership

- *Competency: Resilience and Flexibility*
- *Competency: Plan and Manage Execution*
- *Competency: Make Sound Decisions*

Macro Header: Passionate People Contributing
Core Value Dimension: People Leadership

- *Competency: Coaching and Feedback Skills*
- *Competency: Collaboration*
- *Competency: Customer-Focused Teamwork*
- *Competency: Influence and Persuasion*
- *Competency: Inspire Talent across the Enterprise*

Do you need dimensions? No, not necessarily. Do you need macro headers? No.

What people do and how they do it can identify their attitude.

The Performance Connection

Your performance-based competencies identify what people do on the job from a general, theme-subject perspective. Your performance-based behaviors and practices (the actual items in your survey) measure how effectively the target population performs in each of these theme-subject areas. Performing at a competent level or at any level is contingent upon at least three critical variables: knowledge, skills, and attitudes.

Knowledge is mastery of the background information, the subject matter, the content that you need to know about a subject before you can do something with it. You cannot apply knowledge until you first learn it. You have to know what to do to start your car before you can start the car. Answering the question *What do I know now about this subject?* helps you assess your knowledge. We acquire our knowledge through a variety of means, such as through our senses and by books, observation, experiences, lectures, learning-by-doing, on-the-job training, mentoring, trial and error, mistakes made by others, and so on.

Skills pertain to the practical ability to perform a task after you know what to do or at least where to begin. Skill is demonstrated in the application of what you know. Your skills may be revealed by asking the question *Can I do this (or how well can I do this) based upon what I know?* Your skill to perform can be above expectations, good, bad, acceptable, ineffective, or below expectations, for example. You refine your skill through practice, by learning from your successes and mistakes, and through repetition. Your skill level can identify what additional information or knowledge you may need to know to reach a higher skill level. Your knowledge and willingness to perform at a certain level influences your skill level.

Brain power aside, **attitudes** drive the acquisition and execution (or application) of a person's knowledge. Attitude is the willingness to perform. Attitude is the *I wanna learn it or do it* or *I don't wanna learn it or do it* part of behavior. Attitudes are revealed by answers to the question *To what extent do I want to do this?* You cannot measure attitude.

What people say and how they say it could identify their attitudes towards the person they are communicating with. What one delegates and how one delegates identifies one's attitude towards the other person's competency. Who one invites to key planning meetings identifies one's attitudes towards those invited and, more critically, toward those not invited. People's attitudes can influence the effort and quality of their performance. Past experiences can reinforce one's attitude and performance. How folks respond to someone's performance affects his/her willingness to apply knowledge at a certain skill level and whether (s)he wants to do it again. What people know influences their ability to perform. It can affect their attitude to perform. What they know may not contribute to a higher skill level if past experiences or fear of failure or fear of ridicule is a major influence of their attitude.

Knowledge is nice;

effective application

is nicer.

Riding a Bike

You cannot do anything unless you know how to do it, where to begin, and when and where to continue or stop the process. You cannot ride a bike until you can differentiate a bike from other objects. You cannot ride a bike until you know how and when to get on it and know what its component features — handlebars, brakes, wheels, pedals, gears — are and what each feature does. Your knowledge of those components (competencies) may be nice-to-know information with minimal value until you can apply it and ride the bike with some level of proficiency (skill). Knowing what each component does is nice, as knowledge for knowledge's sake is nice. Applying knowledge so you perform effectively is nicer. You become a competent bike-rider when you actually ride the bike rather than talking about bike riding. You learn how to do this with experience. You learn by reading, watching a video, watching someone else, having someone guide and prompt you through the process and coach you as you fall down after you have run into a tree or something. You become competent at what you do when you can apply what you know at a level that is effective for others. You can call yourself competent, of course, but sometimes the feedback from others carries more social or *psychological* weight.

Attitude and Behavior

This is one of those chicken-or-egg discussions. Does one's attitude drive one's behavior? Or does one's behavior drive one's attitude? Training programs typically focus on behavior and involve exercises that help folks practice the new behaviors. The thinking is that by getting people to do something in a controlled environment and by having them succeed, their attitude towards applying what they have learned to the real world, namely their jobs, will increase. According to this model, actions will affect attitude and encourage folks to repeat newly learned behaviors on a day-to-day basis.

Which comes first, attitude or behavior? It may not matter. When you focus on new behaviors you make it easier for folks to change; when you compare what they have done with what they could be doing differently, you make it easier for them to change. When you identify the how and the why, you make it easier still. They try it. They practice it. They find change relatively easy and painless. They can measure their progress and successes. And the more comfy they are with the new behaviors, the more apt they are to perpetuate those behaviors. An increase in skill level can change attitudes. An increase in their comfort level can change their attitudes. Constant criticism and ridicule can also change behavior, perhaps in ways you may not have intended.

Competencies in Your Assessments

What you reinforce is what you get.

Competencies can include a set of behaviors that describe excellent performance in a particular context (e.g., in a function, role, group of jobs). Behaviors and practices or behavioral indicators are those observable actions that, when executed, demonstrate a person's effectiveness for a particular competency. They may not include (or measure) knowledge but rather *applied* knowledge or behavioral *applications* of that knowledge that produces success. Competencies can include skill levels, manifestations of skills that produce success. They include observable behaviors that could be related to motives (which you may deduce). They are a set of behavioral patterns that someone needs to bring to his or her position, function, or role in order to perform tasks and functions effectively. You can design your assessment to measure how effectively others observe participants applying those behaviors and practices. The sum total of a person's behavioral effectiveness indicates the extent to which that employee is competent in that competency area.

And from a realistic point of view, a competency can simply be a cluster of behaviors or areas that the powers-that-be, aka upper management or the folks who control the gold, identified. This may not have been a terribly collaborative process but more on the order of *Here is what we want you to include. End of conversation.*

Competency Models

A competency model is a guide, a framework, or a roadmap that includes the critical areas that define performance excellence to your employees. Your model can help employees align their career development efforts. You can develop your model from your key business strategies; you can integrate your mission and values; and you can align your training and development initiatives with your model.

There are at least three basic types of competency models.

Functional Models: These describe the behaviors and practices, knowledge, and skills required for exceptional performance for each job or function. Sometimes these types of models define the most important standards of performance or functional excellence. You can easily create a 360-degree assessment for any job or function and align it with your performance appraisal for that job or function.

Core Competency Models: These models identify the critical skills, knowledge, and behaviors that are required for success for all individuals within the organization. While there may be specific critical factors for different jobs or functions, core competency models identify what is common to all employees. They can include standards of performance. Identifying them creates a common language across all levels within the organization.

Role or Positional or Process Models: These models describe the most important or the most critical skills, knowledge, and behaviors for a specific role (e.g., project leader or coach); a specific position (e.g., line supervisor, executive, sales manager); or a process (e.g., problem solving and decision making, Stage-Gate process).

A competency model can organize what you want to measure in your 360-degree assessment. Competency models come in all sizes and shapes. You will see them in outline formats and in circular formats. Some folks focus their efforts creating unique models, such as wheels, pie charts, and pyramids, and so on. There are as many variations as

Models serve as frameworks for discussion.

there are vendors and developers and authors. You can create your models as simply or comprehensively as suits your style and the needs of your audience (e.g., those whose support you need). An outline may suffice. A model based on a Venn diagram may suffice. The format you use can help to illustrate relationships between and among competencies. All models provide a framework for discussion. Here are some examples to get you started.

Your competency model can simply list what you want to measure.
- **Competency:** *Communication*
- **Competency:** *Developing Talent*
- **Competency:** *Flexibility*
- **Competency:** *Functional Expertise*
- **Competency:** *Mission-Oriented*
- **Competency:** *Personal Integrity*
- **Competency:** *Understanding of the Business*

Your competency model can include a header label or dimension so you can align and illustrate relationships among each competency.
1. **Dimension: Business Partner**
- **Competency:** *Mission-Oriented*
- **Competency:** *Understanding of the Business*
- **Competency:** *Articulating Vision*
- **Competency:** *Functional Expertise*

2. **Dimension: People Skills**
- **Competency:** *Communication*
- **Competency:** *Personal Integrity*
- **Competency:** *Developing Talent*
- **Competency:** *Flexibility*

Your competency model can include definitions for each competency.
1. **Dimension: Business Partner**
- **Competency:** *Mission-Oriented*
  Definition: *Understands the goals and purpose of the organization, its products and services, and customers.*
- **Competency:** *Understanding of the Business*
  Definition: *Keeps abreast of trends that have a critical impact on the business.*

- **Competency:** *Articulating Vision*
  Definition: *Communicates a clear vision that inspires and guides employees.*
- **Competency:** *Functional Expertise*
  Definition: *Continuously improves his/her technical and functional knowledge.*

2. **Dimension: People Skills**
- **Competency:** *Communication*
  Definition: *Expresses ideas and exchanges information clearly and effectively.*
- **Competency:** *Personal Integrity*
  Definition: *Applies organizational code of ethics and business conduct.*
- **Competency:** *Developing Talent*
  Definition: *Attracts and develops the right person for the right role or task.*
- **Competency:** *Flexibility*
  Definition: *Responds effectively to change, changing priorities, and ambiguity.*

You may want to expand your outline in order to gather departmental or organizational support. You may want to include sample behaviors-practices. Here are two examples to get you started.

I. CCi Leadership Assessment Survey

Assessment Title: CCi Leadership Assessment Survey
Format: *Web-based*
Description: *This is a 360-degree feedback assessment tool designed for middle- and upper-level managers to help them identify strengths to build upon and areas to develop.*
Dimension: *Intellectual*
- **Competency-Theme:** *Problem Solving—Decision Making*
  Definition: *The ability to analyze a problem, identify its cause, and decide on an appropriate action.*
  Behaviors and Practices for This Competency:
    1. *Gathers the appropriate data to make an informed decision.*
    2. *Provides reasons-rationale for his or her decision.*
    3. *Provides pro-con arguments for his or her decision.*
    4. *Takes risks appropriate to expected benefits, costs.*
    5. *Identifies problems in their early stages.*
    6. *Makes decisions based on sound economic principles, business needs.*
    7. *Identifies alternative solutions when resolving problems.*
    8. *Involves you in the decision-making process.*
    9. *Informs you about what decisions have been made in a timely manner.*
    10. *Supports decisions made by the team.*

Demographic Items:

What is your current location? (Provide choices)

How long have you been in this position? (Provide choices)

How many cross-functional moves have you made? (Provide choices)

Open-Ended Comments:

What could this person START DOING to work more effectively with your internal and/or external customers?

II. CCi Leadership Initiative Survey

Assessment Title: CCi Leadership Initiative

Format: *Web-based*

Description: *A 360-degree assessment designed for personnel in a supervisory-managerial role.*

Dimensions: *4*

Competencies: *13*

Items: *78*

A. Dimension: People Orientation

1. Competency-Theme: Communication

Definition: *The ability to address key issues and share relevant information in a timely and concise manner.*

Lead-in text for each item: *To what extent does this person (the participant) . . .*

a. *Listen to your ideas without interrupting?*

b. *Share information with you in a clear, concise manner?*

c. *Encourage you to contribute your ideas, opinions?*

d. *Communicate ideas in a well-organized manner?*

e. *Summarize key points to verify understanding?*

f. *Provide you with key information when you need it?*

Additional competency definitions could be:

2. Diversity: *The willingness to include individuals with a variety of educational, professional, cultural, life experiences in the group.*

3. Developing Organizational Talent: *The willingness to believe in others' abilities, provide coaching and mentoring, and to help personnel reach their potential.*

4. Team Work: *The willingness to work with others to achieve a common goal.*

5. Leading by Direction: *The ability to provide clear direction to others for what the organization needs to ensure its future success.*

B. Dimension: Task Orientation

    6. Decision Making: *The ability to make effective decisions that provide timely and cost-effective resolution to problems.*

    7. Innovation and Creativity: *The ability to develop and the willingness to apply new ideas and practices.*

    8. Planning and Organizing: *The ability to plan and organize work and set measurable goals for a work group or project.*

C. Dimension: Results Orientation

    9. Business Savvy: *The ability to implement the right actions in order to succeed in the business environment with customers and suppliers.*

    10. Financial Analysis—Budgeting: *The ability to understand and effectively utilize financial reports and controls.*

    11. Quality of Work Results: *The ability to produce high quality work (e.g., research, procedures, services, products) consistently over time.*

D. Dimension: Self-Orientation

    12. Continuous Learning: *The willingness to develop to his or her full potential through ongoing learning and development.*

    13. Adaptability: *The ability and willingness to adjust to pressure situations and rapidly changing business conditions, and to implement new procedures and processes.*

You can create competency models for any purpose or target population. If you wanted to create a competency model for leadership, you could create the model based upon any of these demographics or themes:

By position or title, e.g., Team Leader, First Line Supervisor, Middle Manager, Executive, General Manager, Director, CFO, or CIO.

By function or department, e.g., Accounting—Finance, Human Resources, Marketing, Sales, Product Management, Customer Service, Information Systems, Legal, Engineering, Technical Service, Training, or Installation and Post-Sales Support.

By applications or theme, e.g., Change Leadership, Team Leadership, Supervisory Leadership, Sales Management Leadership, High Potential Leadership, Succession Planning, Influencing Skills, Relationship Skills, Task Skills, Project Management Leadership, Coaching Skills, or Mentoring Skills.

By geographical location, e.g., United States (or your specific country), North America, Mexico and/or Latin America, Europe, Asia, South East Asia, or Pacific Region.

The Best Model

First, there is no one best competency model for leadership or sales or team building. There may be models that are more complete or more comprehensive or more applicable to your situation, yet best is only best until the next best thing comes along. Be patient; next month will bring a new best model! Second, generally speaking, people see their competency model as better than someone else's model. Okay. Third, review the competencies listed in any model along with how that author defines each competency. The competencies may not represent what you want to measure or what you feel is relevant to your organization. The model may be a terrific model according to the vendor, but it might be (by your requirements) not relevant to your target population or organization in particular. Ergo, it is not best for you. Will your vendor or survey developer modify the model to meet your requirements? That would be a good thing. There are as many best core competency models for a best leadership instrument as there are authors and vendors. So, here is our best.

We developed and marketed the Leadership Assessment Survey (LAS) in 1982 and originally marketed it under the title Leadership Development Profile (LDP). The LAS was the first instrument designed for people in managerial and leadership functions around the world. We revised this survey over the years. The current version includes ninety-six behaviors and practices linked to sixteen critical core competencies. These competencies represent the basic performance competencies for effective managerial personnel. The LAS applies to people who are in managerial positions, such as supervisors, managers, and executive-level personnel in business, education, and governmental organizations. The LAS continues to be our most popular and most comprehensive assessment of the one hundred-plus other performance-based 360-degree assessments we market around the world. The primary competency model for the Leadership Assessment Survey is

The best model is the one being promoted by that author.

structured by dimensions and core competencies, which are defined for the raters.

CCi Leadership Assessment Survey (Primary Model)

Dimension: Personal Values
Core Competencies
1. **Initiative and Risk Taking:** *The ability to demonstrate individual drive and accept responsibility for his/her actions.*
2. **Personal Integrity:** *The ability to gain the trust and confidence of others by interacting in a fair and honest manner.*
3. **Vision:** *The ability to create and describe an ideal state or condition and align others toward its accomplishment.*
4. **Quality of Results:** *The commitment to produce high quality work (research, procedures, services, products) consistently, over time.*
5. **Empowerment:** *The willingness to create a work environment in which people are encouraged to develop their full potential.*

Dimension: Performance Management
Core Competencies
6. **Communicating:** *The ability to express ones' self clearly and to listen effectively to others.*
7. **Delegating:** *The ability to assign work, clarify expectations, and define how individual performance will be measured.*
8. **Motivating:** *The ability to create a satisfying work environment that encourages others to work towards achieving group goals.*
9. **Coaching:** *The ability to provide feedback and offer support when people are confronted with performance problems.*

Dimension: Task Management
Core Competencies
10. **Planning and Goal Setting:** *The ability to plan and organize work and set realistic, measurable objectives for a work unit or project.*
11. **Problem Solving and Decision Making:** *The ability to analyze a situation, identify alternative solutions, and make appropriate decisions.*
12. **Creativity and Innovation:** *The ability to develop and apply new and innovative ideas and practices.*
13. **Technical Competency:** *The commitment to keep current technically and perform work in a knowledgeable manner.*

Dimension: Group Dynamics
  Core Competencies
  14. Diversity: *The willingness to work with individuals and integrate the differences that exist among others.*
  15. Team Work: *The ability to work effectively with others to achieve a common goal.*

Dimension: Guiding Others
  Core Competency
  16. Mentoring: *The willingness to support others in their personal and professional development.*

Now you may have thought about different labels for these dimensions or competencies and different definitions. Fine! Every author has their own labels. The key here is to use language applicable to your organization, without sounding overly woo-woo-whiz-bang. Define what you mean so other people know what you mean. That works! If you do not define each competency, each rater will define it from his or her own perspective. That does not work.

Competency Model Options for a Leadership Assessment Survey

Contrary to what you may have heard, competency models are not cast in concrete. You can change and reorganize your model depending on your focus. There is nothing sacred about the sequence of the competencies in your model. And while the structure of your model may change, the items that measure each competency do not need to change. For example, if your intent is to create an assessment organized by general *task* and *relationship* competencies, one option to the CCi *Leadership Assessment Survey* (primary model) could be constructed like this:

Leadership Assessment Survey (modified for task-relationships)

Dimension: Task Competencies
- *Creativity and Innovation*
- *Initiative and Risk Taking*
- *Planning and Goal Setting*
- *Problem Solving and Decision Making*
- *Quality of Results*
- *Technical Competency*

Dimension: Relationship Competencies
- *Coaching*
- *Communicating*
- *Delegating*
- *Diversity*
- *Empowerment*
- *Mentoring*
- *Motivating*
- *Personal Integrity*
- *Teamwork*
- *Vision*

If your focus is career development, you could reorganize our primary model like this:

Leadership Assessment Survey (modified for career development)

Dimension: Thinking *(e.g., how participants process information)*
- *Creativity and Innovation*
- *Planning and Goal Setting*
- *Problem Solving and Decision Making*

Dimension: Performance *(e.g., how participants conduct themselves on the job)*
- *Initiative and Risk Taking*
- *Quality of Results*
- *Technical Competency*

Dimension: Building Relationships *(e.g., how participants establish rapport and trust)*

- *Coaching*
- *Communicating*
- *Delegating*
- *Diversity*
- *Empowerment*
- *Mentoring*
- *Motivating*
- *Personal Integrity*
- *Teamwork*
- *Vision*

If your focus is on team leadership for the team leader or inter-departmental effectiveness, an option could be:

Leadership Assessment Survey (modified for team leadership)

Dimension: Analysis and Execution

- *Creativity and Innovation*
- *Planning and Goal Setting*
- *Problem Solving and Decision Making*
- *Technical Competency*

Dimension: Personal Drive and Focus

- *Initiative and Risk Taking*
- *Quality of Results*
- *Personal Integrity*
- *Vision*

Dimension: Supporting Others

- *Diversity*
- *Mentoring*
- *Teamwork*

Dimension: Developing Others

- *Coaching*
- *Communication*
- *Delegating*
- *Empowerment*
- *Motivating*

Competency Application: Exercise

How would you organize these sixteen competencies for your organization and your assessment's focus? Would you include dimensions? Review the sixteen competencies on the previous pages, and make any revisions for your compency model.

Which Competency Goes First?

Someone above you may want you to justify why you have selected the sequence of competencies that you've chosen. When you create an assessment, you list one competency before another. Sounds simple enough. But which should go first and why? Does order matter? The sequence of each skill-competency-theme is irrelevant unless you want people to believe that some competencies are more important from a procedural point of view or that one competency is dependent on another. For example, to what extent would you present these competencies in this particular sequence—communicating, delegating, empowerment, motivating, coaching? If so, why? What other sequence might you use and why?

There may be a logical sequence from a training perspective. Some internal folks prefer to design their assessments to match the modular sequence of their training programs. That's fine. This allows you to cover the feedback for each competency as you present that corresponding training module in your program. Yet to what extent would you actually apply these in that logical sequence on the job? Order, hierarchy, or sequence may be important in a textbook or in a training session, but perhaps may not be applicable in the real world. So does the sequence really matter in your assessment? Or is knowing how to do something and when to apply this knowledge more critical? The sequence of how you present each competency can be logical (e.g., these themes fit with that dimension or they are listed in alphabetical order). Some suggest listing them in a sequence of importance to the organization. Okay, but whose sequence of importance is that? Is it that of the folks at the top, the folks who are below them, or the trainers who conduct training in a specific sequence? Which competency goes first? It may not matter, really. What may matter is to group competencies by what they have in common, e.g., competencies by task, by relationship, by people skills, by developing others, and so on. What may matter more is that you are able to justify the sequence to others, just in case.

Getting to Your Uniqueness

Some folks see themselves and/or their organizations as unique. Let's assume your target population is mid-managerial personnel. Identify what you think is unique about your organization and what you want to measure for this target population. Do not include the specific products and services you offer. Group what you think is unique about your organization into two columns: task competencies-skills (thing stuff) and relationship competencies-skills (people stuff).

Uniqueness Application: Exercise I

Task Competencies	Relationship Competencies

What did you include in each? My guess is that you identified things like communicating, being a leader, assigning work and priorities, handling conflict, motivating people, helping people perform, making decisions, working with others, and so on. Now think of an organization in which effective managers do not also need to communicate, or be leaders, or assign work, or motivate people, and so on. You probably can't. While it may be true that your managers may not do these things effectively, it is also true that all effective managers need to communicate and make decisions and delegate and motivate and work cooperatively with others regardless of their current levels of effectiveness. You haven't yet identified what is unique about your organization if you've stopped at listing competencies such as these.

Often when people talk about what is unique, they are thinking about the politics of their organization or the technical aspects required to do specific jobs within their organizations or the way a piece of paper moves from one desk to another. Is your organization bureaucratic? Bureaucracy is not unique. Is there something about your bureaucratic organization that is unique? What is it? Identify it. Does your organization function as a matrix organization? What is unique about how that process works in your organization? Is there something unique about how your salespeople interact with your clients? Is there something unique about your sales cycle? Is that what you want to measure? People do the same things in all organizations—they talk to people, they talk about people, they think, they make decisions, they do stuff, they whine and complain, they get at the core of an issue very quickly, or not, they engage in office politics, they form alliances and networks, they are cooperative, they are disruptive, they are great to work with, they do things effectively, and they do things that are borderline dopey. But your organization may do these things differently than others do.

Some organizations are spread around the globe. A manager from one location may manage folks from a totally different culture. Do you work in a virtual organization? Do employees work at home or out of their home? There are special issues about distant or virtual organizations that could be unique. What are they? As you list aspects that are truly unique, are you identifying areas that are, well, not unique? For example, do your employees still need to talk to one another and make decisions and do stuff and solve problems? Is there something unique about how they do these things, regardless of whether they work at home or in an office setting with others? Does conflict arise and if so, among whom? Are some employees self-starters? Are some employees highly motivated while others need to be gently prodded just to breathe?

Uniqueness can be a status symbol, a source of pride. To be unique means that you are different from others, but being different can be scary if being different is considered a negative. Your being different can be a scary nightmare to your competitors, especially if they have to chase after you just to remain competitive. Before you talk to a vendor about your uniqueness, you'll want to identify what is unique about your organization or a special target population. Write it down. Share this with others within the organization. Decide if what folks think is unique is worth measuring. Collaborate with others to capture that uniqueness, to measure key aspects of that uniqueness in a proprietary assessment designed for you.

Keep in mind that your organization may be less unique than you think. It may be more relevant to think about what you want to measure and why from a performance point of view. This may not be as sexy or cerebral. When it comes to two people working together, many of the issues are the same from one organization to the next, from one culture to the next, regardless of discipline and culture and location and educational level.

Uniqueness Application: Exercise II

What is unique about your organization that you may want to explore with your favorite vendor or explore in an assessment?

The Issue of Localization

Uniqueness and localization can be issues between countries and cultures. Organizations with multiple offices in multiple countries face barriers when they attempt to adapt any assessment from one culture to another, from one language set to another. Many of these barriers do not apply to performance-based 360-degree assessments. If you are a multi-national organization or if you want to implement an assessment created in one country, say the United States, and want to administer it within a different country, say Korea, you need to think about the localization issues. One such issue involves receiving feedback from multiple sources, specifically from people below the participant, i.e., direct reports. In some cultures, providing this upward feedback was or still is seen as disrespectful to that participant. The feedback can be seen as criticism rather than as constructive or informative. That aspect of localization focuses on who should be providing the feedback and for what purpose. Does this aspect of localization apply to you?

Language is another issue related to localization. Some English words, even when translated, might not have meaning to the raters. The use of jargon was (and still is) widespread in many surveys, and some assessment developers use different words to separate themselves from others. Now if you develop an instrument solely for your organization, perhaps using your jargon is a non-issue. But when you transport that same instrument outside your four walls to other cultures, you may have a problem. Every culture has its own jargon. When you eliminate jargon from the questions in your surveys, the issue of localization typically does not come up; if it does, it is easily overcome. Drop the jargon.

And be sensitive to spelling differences. The British version of English substitutes the letter s for z in words like "organisation" and includes the letter *u* in words like "behaviour," or the letter *e* is added to words such as "judgement." Spelling changes should be localized as a matter of grammatical correctness and courtesy for countries that use the British version of English.

Localizing words to a country is not confined to English-speaking countries, of course. Localizing words does not apply to jargon only. For example, speakers in Spain typically use the word "conducir" (to drive) when referring to driving an automobile, while other Spanish speaking countries tend to use the word "manejar." In Spain, the word "plantilla" often identifies someone who is a direct report. Spanish-speaking folks in the Americas tend not to use that word. "Plantilla" means the bottom of a shoe. "Plantilla" and its symbolism in this context tends to smack of "los conquistadores" and colonialism. It is legitimate and necessary to localize words to the local culture. Your assessment will have greater credibility when you make these kinds of changes.

Another issue of localization centers around the competencies in your 360-degree assessment. The wording of the competency is an issue, and by eliminating jargon and esoteric labels you can easily overcome any concerns about whether your assessment will apply to another culture. Not too many years ago, competencies labeled "empowerment," "vision," and "diversity" (among others) had less or little meaning in some countries. The key is to examine your competencies. Depending on the instrument you have created or are about to purchase, if it includes boiler-plate competency labels, such as "communication" and "delegation" and "problem solving" and "decision making" and "personal integrity" and "coaching" and "motivation," for example, you have to ask yourself whether these are the competencies that any effective manager (or whomever) needs. Regardless of the country culture or organizational culture that you are a part of, ask yourself whether managers would be considered effective if they lacked these competencies? If managerial personnel lacked these competencies, how effective would they be, for example, with their direct reports? How effective would your organization be if your managers were not effective in these (and other) areas? You cannot identify an effective manager in any type of organization who does not need to be effective in these basic areas. If that manager manages people, they have to communicate and delegate and coach and motivate and resolve problems effectively. Localization for these kinds of universal competencies is a non-issue. Localization for pop-jargon-campy competencies will continue to be an issue.

People need to be effective with the basics first. The whiz-bang-woo-woo comes later.

Whose Assessment—Theirs or Yours?

Should you build or buy? You can save time and money and use a generic 360-degree survey. You can skip the critical incident discussions, brainstorming, and all the analytical work when you use an off-the-shelf assessment. You might get results you can use, but probably also results that come under the category of "so what." You can also create a proprietary instrument for your own organization. This *should* yield much more relevant information for your organization. The themes you include should apply to your organization. Don't be concerned about fads; be concerned about what competencies apply to the people in your organization the most. You can then decide which is the most appropriate for your organization—a generic or a custom product.

If you believe your organization is unique, benchmarking may be irrelevant.

Benchmarking

You can benchmark your organization against other organizations. Some folks prefer to do what other folks do, and some folks are curious about comparing their folks with folks from other organizations. Benchmarking is one way to do that. At its simplest, benchmarking is a means of improving oneself by learning from others, *as long as you are willing to implement needed changes.* It is often helpful to compare yourself to what others have done and compare your results to their results. Typically, benchmarking focuses on processes, the process of measuring one's company's methods, products, services, business practices, and procedures against others in one's industry or in the workplace in general. Benchmarking has been applied to managerial-leadership competencies as well. As a mode of comparison, benchmarking assumes there is (or are) best practitioners against whom one can compare. The key is to compare your company with those companies that consistently outperform and distinguish themselves in the same measurement areas that are relevant to your organization. Benchmarking can identify performance gaps. It can help organizations identify new ways or best practices for doing something.

So, should you consider benchmarking? In some cases, benchmarking can be nice to have. If you are the top competitor in your industry, if you are the leader, then benchmarking to others who are not as effective as you is likely a waste of time. Don't forget: Your competition is trying to catch you. Why would you want to compare your organization with less effective organizations? You would be lowering your standards and performance to the benchmark. Benchmarking may sometimes be campy, but keep in mind that what works for organizations in general may not work for your own organization. Benchmarking your organization to others does not take into account your culture, your level of bureaucracy, innovation, entrepreneurialism, and so on. Benchmarking can be a starting point. Benchmarking may not be the comparative model relevant to your organization. Benchmarking may not be relevant for leading organizations. You decide whether it is relevant for you. You decide where you are in relation to your competitors.

Do you need a competency model? No, not necessarily, but coming up with one is a handy way to organize what you want to measure and to talk about it in a structured format.

Finding Your Competencies

"Hey," you say, *"I can do this."* So begin. Sometimes it is easy to identify what you need to measure. You may have decided to start by identifying competencies. In the process, doubtless, you will find yourself talking about behaviors. Regardless, the competencies you ultimately select need to apply to your organization. They should tie into your other initiatives, such as your training programs, performance appraisal processes, and career development programs, for example, that reinforce what you are doing now or what you could be doing to create a more viable organization. Consider these questions to get you started.

- *Do you want to measure competencies that your people need today?*
- *Do you want to measure competencies that your people will need tomorrow to help your organization become more competitive, more customer-oriented, or more people-oriented?*
- *Do you want to include competencies in your assessment because that is what you think you should include because others include them?*
- *Do you include them because that is what your organization needs and that is what you are prepared to develop and reinforce?*
- *What competencies do you want people to focus on for interdepartmental effectiveness?*
- *What competencies are most critical to your organization?*

Venn Diagrams

You can create a set of competencies for a single target population or for all (or almost all) employees within your organization, business unit, or functional area. Let's assume that you need to develop multiple instruments for different functions, job titles, or locations. You could do this for any job description. When you create multiple instruments, identify what is common to all employees, regardless of function, title, location, and so on.

Create a Venn diagram to illustrate which competencies intersect or overlap. A Venn diagram clarifies the relationship between the parts of a whole. It uses circles or ovals to represent sets and their relationships. In a Venn diagram the areas that overlap are your core competencies across all (or almost all) employee demographics. The competencies that do not overlap and apply to a specific function become unique to that function. You can then create an assessment that includes both the core competencies and those unique to that function.

Where should you begin? Ask yourself, "What does any effective supervisor, manager, or executive do within this organization?"

Your initial efforts are for getting it down, not for getting it good.

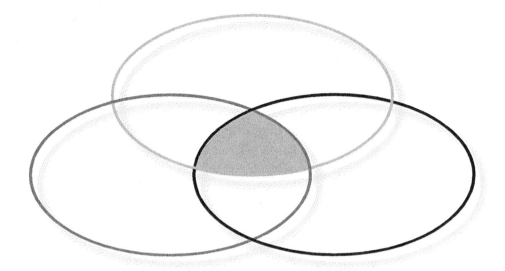

- *Do they need to delegate tasks and responsibilities to others?*
- *Do they need to coach people to perform up to (or exceed) expectations?*
- *Do they need to motivate and inspire and persuade others to do something, such as buying into a new project or process or procedure?*
- *Do they need to resolve problems and make decisions?*
- *Do they need to work with others in a cooperative and effective way?*
- *Do they need to be trustworthy?*
- *Do they need to show personal initiative and drive?*
- *Do they need to understand financial information?*

If these areas apply to all people in a managerial role, include them in your core competency model. You may find that not all managerial personnel in all functions need to coach or motivate. You may discover that an effective alternative in some functions or at some levels is to YST (Yell, Scream, and Threaten). In this case, coaching and motivation are not core competencies for all managerial personnel, but only those personnel in these functions or those locations or who manages those kinds of direct reports, while YST is applicable to just that function or that location or folks who manage that kind of direct report.

Using a Venn diagram or similar tool helps you see what is common to all and what is unique to specific functions or roles. Look for similarities among each function or role. This provides you with at least three design options:

1. *Design one assessment that includes the core competencies that apply to all personnel;*
2. *Design multiple assessments that include competencies relevant to each separate function, title, or role; or*
3. *Design multiple assessments for each function, title, or role that include the core competencies and those competencies relevant to each function, title, or role.*

Each option allows you to easily link your performance-based 360-degree assessment with your performance appraisal process or career development track, for example. You will reinforce a common language employees understand. Link your assessment language to the language in your training and development programs. When you integrate and link performance issues, you create a common language set for development. Employees understand the relevance of assessment, training and development, appraisals, and compensation. They understand what you expect of them. They understand the connections.

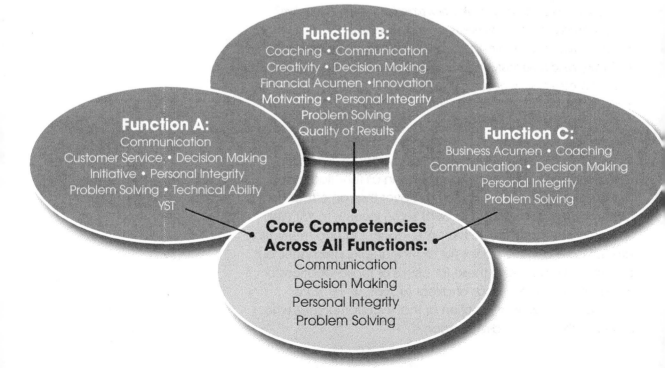

Function B:
Coaching • Communication
Creativity • Decision Making
Financial Acumen • Innovation
Motivating • Personal Integrity
Problem Solving
Quality of Results

Function A:
Communication
Customer Service • Decision Making
Initiative • Personal Integrity
Problem Solving • Technical Ability
YST

Function C:
Business Acumen • Coaching
Communication • Decision Making
Personal Integrity
Problem Solving

**Core Competencies
Across All Functions:**
Communication
Decision Making
Personal Integrity
Problem Solving

Spreadsheets

Venn diagrams are one option. There are others. For example, you may prefer a snappy spreadsheet to identify what competencies are common to each functional area. Here are two examples:

BY COMPETENCY							
	Communication	Customer Service	Decision Making	Integrity	Problem Solving	YST	Team Work
FUNCTIONAL AREA:							
A	X		X	X	X		X
B	X		X	X	X		X
C	X		X	X	X		X
D	X	X	X	X	X	X	X
E	X			X		X	

BY FUNCTIONAL AREA					
	Function A	Function B	Function C	Function D	Function E
COMPETENCY:					
Communication	X	X	X	X	X
Customer Service				X	
Decision Making	X	X	X	X	
Integrity	X	X	X	X	X
Problem Solving	X	X	X	X	
YST				X	X
Team Work	X	X	X	X	

One of our chemical manufacturing clients hired us to create four proprietary instruments. One instrument was for individual contributors, another for first line supervisors, the third for managers, and the fourth for executives. The client helped us identify those competencies that were common to all employees. We included these present-state baseline competencies in each assessment. We also identified and included future-state competencies, competencies employees would need to compete more effectively tomorrow. We included a third set of competencies unique to each target population that focused on that population's respective functions or roles.

Critical Incident Method

You can identify competencies yourself, or you can involve others. Getting the input of others can be a smart thing. But you need to be smart in getting that input. During your session, think in terms of critical incidents. Suppose you want to create an assessment for your sales personnel. Each person in your session should be able to . . .

Identify an incident that had a very positive influence on the outcome of the interaction between the salesperson and a customer. For example:

Resolved customer complaint

Closed the sale

Uncovered new applications for a product the customer has purchased

Identified new client applications for a product the customer has not purchased

Describe the incident. Answer these kinds of questions, for example:

What did the salesperson do to resolve the complaint?

What did the salesperson do to close the sale?

What did the salesperson do to uncover those new applications?

Describe the activities or events that led up to the incident. Answer these questions, for example:

Why did the complaint occur in the first place?

How did the salesperson close the sale?

How did the salesperson uncover the needs or applications?

List the ways the incident helped to secure a positive outcome for the salesperson, the organization, and the customer. For example, did it have these results:

Satisfied customer

Increased the order

Customer purchased new product(s)

Referred salesperson to another (department, company, friend)

If possible, schedule multiple sessions with the same types of folks in each session. Schedule sessions with only salespeople and only with sales managers, for example. As you progress through this process, you will identify recurring themes-competencies. Behaviors and practices will emerge. As they do, you will be able to organize and sort through them and link them to each competency. You can then prioritize and refine what you have.

Alternative Methods

Some folks may not be able to think of a really important, relevant incident. An alternative way to finding your core competencies is to consider the following process. As when doing any brainstorming process, record each idea without any initial judgment. Writing things down helps folks remember what was said. Reading it helps folks think of other ideas. Posting or projecting the list on the wall keeps the process moving. In multiple sessions you . . .

Get it down:
Brainstorm what salespeople say an effective salesperson does
Brainstorm what others see effective salespeople do
Brainstorm what external people see an effective salesperson doing (or should do)

Organize it:
Group common behaviors under common subject areas or themes
Prioritize the more critical behaviors from the nice-to-haves

Name it:
Create a competency label for each subject area or theme

Finalize it:
Refine each competency label so people understand what you want to measure
Refine each core behavior so it is observable and measurable

Can you do all of this in a single session? Sure! Sometimes, however, the length of a session can approach that of a short-term career. Sometimes stepping back and having a day or so to think can be more productive and beneficial. The process works both ways. You can identify competencies first, then identify the core behaviors that measure each competency; or you can identify core behaviors first, then link them to their appropriate competencies later. Consider these questions as a starting point:

- *What do highly effective salespeople do as they perform their jobs?* (Do they present products and services? Resolve problems? Ask questions? Identify solutions to customer problems—concerns? Handle objections?)
- *How do highly effective salespeople perform their jobs?* (Do they make face-to-face calls? Do they train customers to use products and services effectively?)
- *How would you describe people who perform in an exceptional manner?* (Do they follow up after the sale? Do they help build the customers' business? Do they provide technical information that is easy to understand?)
- *What are the top five qualities an effective salesperson must have?* (Are communication skills on the list? Product knowledge? Competitive and Market knowledge?)
- *What could our salespeople start doing, stop doing, and/or continue doing to interact more effectively with our external customers and our internal resources?*

Ask yourself (and others) one or more of these basic questions when you want to identify the behaviors for your potential core competencies or themes:

- *What do highly effective salespeople do when they handle objections?*
- *How do highly effective salespeople communicate with customers?*
- *How would you describe someone who provided exceptional customer service?*
- *How does an effective salesperson demonstrate products and services?*

Another option is to focus on performance objectives and measurement standards. Consider these four basic questions as a starting point:

- *What was the person expected to accomplish?*
- *How was the accomplishment to be measured?*
- *What is expected to achieve satisfactory (or excellent) performance?*
- *How were the expectations (goals) met?*

Keep in mind that, regardless of the method you use to identify your competencies or behaviors and practices, your initial goal is *to get it all down,* not to get it good. Fine tuning and getting into the details comes later.

Okay, so you got it down. You have a long list. Now you need to get it good.

The first step (believe it or not) is to shorten your list. You need to eliminate overlaps and redundancies. Narrow your list to those critical core competencies (or behaviors) that apply to your target population. Gather key personnel and have them identify them from their point of view. One method is to create index cards with the name of one competency per card. Each person receives his/her own stack of these cards with the instructions that (s)he must create three equal competency piles:

- **Must-haves** and high importance or critical value
- **Should-haves** and medium importance
- **Nice-to-haves** and low importance or critical value

You need to end up with piles of equal height. If people believe that everything is a must-have and of high critical value, then you end up without any differentiation. That is, you will end up with zip.

First, compare the must-have and high critical value piles of each person. What is common to everyone? Which competencies appear in more must-have high critical value piles (i.e., what is the frequency of occurrence)? The focus should be on what people see as critical, not on what people see as least important. However, if things are not as clear-cut, then identify those competencies that received the least number of votes. Eliminate those from any further stacking and ordering. Then repeat the process with the remaining competencies. Create three equal piles with the same criteria as your goal.

The process might seem laborious. Maybe what is critical is obvious to everyone. Yet getting people to sort through and consider all of the options and make decisions about what is critical is a necessary step. There is no magic number of competencies that you need to end up with. What is essential is to identify those areas that are critical to your assessment in today's or tomorrow's environment, or for meeting whatever goals you've set for this instrument.

By the way, you may decide not to solicit feedback from customers (internal or external) at this stage. Yet without multiple sources your input could be biased, so you might want to reconsider. Why? Well, most sales training programs include something about handling objections, asking for the order, knowing what types of questions to ask, when to ask those questions, making a (canned) presentation, and so on. This may be all nice and good, but do customers really care about those issues compared to a salesperson's ability and willingness to listen, to treat customers with respect, treat customers as partners, understand customer needs, and to provide a product or service that meets that need?

My point is this: Is your information-gathering process slanted towards what internally you (and the power people) believe are effective behaviors, or what the recipients, the customers, the end-users want to see from your salespeople? There can be critical differences. Involve your customers, internal and external!

Suppose the following behaviors and practices result from your brainstorming session. What would you add, modify, or drop? What priority or degree of critical value would each behavior get for your organization? Which behaviors would you cluster under a specific competency? What competency labels would you use?

Brainstorming Application: Exercise I
What does an effective salesperson do?

BEHAVIORS AND PRACTICES	IMPORTANCE OR PRIORITY	YOUR COMPETENCY LABEL
Calls on customers regularly		
Identifies objectives of sales call to the customer		
Asks questions		Communication?
Listens		Listening (Communication?)
Handles objections		
Asks for the order		
Completes paperwork		Administration?
Makes 8 sales calls per day		
Follows up after the sale		Self-Motivation?
Resolves customer problems		
Makes presentations		
Has initiative		Self-Motivation?
Is professional		
Knows the products, services		Technical Acumen?
Is reliable		Integrity?
Identifies customer needs		
Analyzes the situation		
Develops customer loyalty		
Handles technical questions		Technical Knowledge? Communication?
Submits expense reports		
Has a professional image		
Organizes who to call on and when (how often)		
Conducts demonstrations		
Trains customers to use our products		

Now suppose the following competencies were identified in your brainstorming session. What behaviors and practices for your sales assessment would you add to each competency? What competency labels would you use instead of those listed here?

Brainstorming Application: Exercise II
What does an effective salesperson do?

YOUR COMPETENCIES	BEHAVIORS AND PRACTICES: WHAT DOES AN EFFECTIVE SALESPERSON DO IN EACH OF THESE COMPETENCIES?
Account Service	
Customer Service	
Establishing Rapport	
Handle Objections	
Order Processing	
Product Knowledge	
Professionalism and Image	
Selling Skills	
Territory Management	

Competency Selection Application: Exercise

Have you decided what competencies to include in your performance-based assessment? If not, consider the following examples as a starting point. Select those competencies that you believe could apply to all or most personnel. Consider these your core competencies. Then identify a specific target population or function and identify what additional competencies would apply only to them. Upon completion, you will have two assessments: core and functional. Change the wording of the competencies you select to reflect your organization as necessary.

IF YOU WANT AN ASSESSMENT FOR LEADERSHIP DEVELOPMENT . . .	WHICH OF THESE COMPETENCIES WOULD APPLY TO YOUR ORGANIZATION?
	Building Relationships
	Business Acumen
	Client Relationship
	Coaching
	Communication
	Conflict Resolution
	Coordinating
	Creative Problem Solving
	Creativity and Innovation
	Decision Making
	Delegating
	Developing People
	Diversity
	Emotional Intelligence
	Financial Acumen
	Flexibility (or Versatility)
	Interpersonal Skills
	Leadership Abilities
	Leading Teams
	Mentoring
	Motivation
	Performance Management
	Personal Integrity
	Problem Solving
	Professionalism
	Project Management
	Self-Direction
	Stress Management
	Team Building
	Teamwork
	Technical Competency
	Time Management
	Vision

Consider the following target populations and competencies for your feedback project. What would you select? What else would you include?

IF YOU WANT AN ASSESSMENT FOR HR PERSONNEL . . .	WHICH OF THESE COMPETENCIES WOULD APPLY TO YOUR ORGANIZATION?
	Business Partner
	Change Agent
	Leadership
	Meeting Client Needs
	Taking the Initiative

IF YOU WANT AN ASSESSMENT FOR ADMINISTRATIVE ASSISTANTS . . .	WHICH OF THESE COMPETENCIES WOULD APPLY TO YOUR ORGANIZATION?
	Execution
	Initiative
	Self-Management
	Technical Competency

IF YOU WANT AN ASSESSMENT FOR MANAGEMENT DEVELOPMENT . . .	WHICH OF THESE COMPETENCIES WOULD APPLY TO YOUR ORGANIZATION?
	Analytical Reasoning
	Communication
	Emotional Intelligence
	Interpersonal Sensitivity
	Lateral Thinking
	Leadership
	Motivating Others
	Planning
	Problem Solving and Decision Making

IF YOU WANT AN ASSESSMENT FOR CUSTOMER SERVICE PERSONNEL . . .	WHICH OF THESE COMPETENCIES WOULD APPLY TO YOUR ORGANIZATION?
	Communication Skills
	Emotional Intelligence
	Follow-Up, Follow-Through
	Handling Irate Customers
	Identifying Problems, Concerns
	Resolving Problems
	Service Excellence
	Value Added Service

IF YOU WANT AN ASSESSMENT FOR TEAM BUILDING . . .	WHICH OF THESE COMPETENCIES WOULD APPLY TO YOUR ORGANIZATION?
	Commitment
	Communication
	Customer Relations
	Flexibility
	Integrity
	Organization and Focus
	Problem Solving and Decision Making
	Quality of Work
	Supporting Others
	Technical Competency
	Valuing Differences

IF YOU WANT AN ASSESSMENT FOR PUBLIC SERVICE OFFICIALS . . .	WHICH OF THESE COMPETENCIES WOULD APPLY TO YOUR ORGANIZATION?
	Budgeting and Financial Acumen
	Citizen Participation
	Communication
	Diversity
	Financial Analysis
	Functional Expertise
	Human Resource Management
	Initiative and Risk Taking
	Media-Presentation Skills
	Personal Integrity
	Planning
	Policy Facilitation
	Public Relations
	Quality Assurance
	Staff Effectiveness
	Strategic Planning
	Vision and Innovation

IF YOU WANT AN ASSESSMENT FOR INDIVIDUAL CONTRIBUTORS . . .	WHICH OF THESE COMPETENCIES WOULD APPLY TO YOUR ORGANIZATION?
	Communication
	Creativity and Innovation
	Diversity
	Initiative and Risk Taking
	Personal Integrity
	Planning and Execution
	Problem Solving and Decision Making
	Quality of Work Results
	Team Work
	Technical Competenc

IF YOU WANT AN ASSESSMENT FOR STAGE GATE—TECHNICAL FOCUS ...	WHICH OF THESE COMPETENCIES WOULD APPLY TO YOUR ORGANIZATION?
	Application Testing
	Assess Feasibility Project Plans
	Follow-Up Support
	Identify Process Concept

IF YOU WANT AN ASSESSMENT FOR UPPER LEVEL EDUCATORS—ADMINISTRATORS ...	WHICH OF THESE COMPETENCIES WOULD APPLY TO YOUR ORGANIZATION?
	Collaboration
	Communicate Expectations
	Communication Skills
	Decisiveness
	Frame Academic—Department Goals
	Influence and Integrity
	Interpersonal Relations
	Leadership
	Leadership Challenge
	Maintain Visibility
	Personal Organization
	Planning
	Problem Solving and Decision Making
	Reinforce Excellence
	Reinforce Learning

IF YOU WANT AN ASSESSMENT FOR SALES MANAGEMENT ...	WHICH OF THESE COMPETENCIES WOULD APPLY TO YOUR ORGANIZATION?
	Branch Office Leadership
	Business Development
	Business Planning
	Commitment to Quality
	Communication Skills
	Diversity
	Flexibility
	Integrity
	Individual Knowledge
	Influencing Others
	Maintaining Profitability
	Managing Performance
	Problem Solving and Decision Making
	Process Improvement
	Recruiting Qualified Personnel
	Succession Planning
	Team Building

IF YOU WANT AN ASSESSMENT FOR SALES DEVELOPMENT (Account Executives and Salespeople) . . .	WHICH OF THESE COMPETENCIES WOULD APPLY TO YOUR ORGANIZATION?
	Account Development
	Account Penetration
	Active Listening
	Customer Service
	Developing Partnerships
	Establishing Rapport
	Handling Concerns
	Personal Initiative
	Personal Integrity and Image
	Presenting to Groups
	Product—Market Knowledge
	Professionalism and Image
	Selling Skills
	Timeliness

Define Your Competencies

Define what you mean so others know what you mean.

You may know what you want to measure and include in your 360-degree survey. Define each competency as part of your design or development process. Definitions help clarify each competency. Ask ten people to define "empowerment" and you will probably get ten different definitions. You need to define what you (or your committee) mean by each competency. Now, you do not always need to define your competencies to raters in the final assessment. However, you need to do so if you include an "importance rating" section. If you do not define what you intend to assess, raters will be confused about what you are referring to. During your design process, consider defining each competency to keep your efforts focused.

Identify your core competencies so the people helping you stay focused on what your design-development group means when they discuss each competency. Then, develop specific behaviors that measure each competency based upon your definition. Your definitions drive what you want to measure. When you define your competencies, the behaviors-practices that make up the body of your assessment should not repeat all of the elements of your definition, but rather expand upon the definitions by identifying observable events-actions-performance.

Here are some sample definitions of selected competencies to get you thinking. These definitions may work for you. If they don't, modify them to suit your purposes and intent.

Defining Competencies Application: Exercise

DEFINITIONS TO CONSIDER . . .	HOW WOULD YOU RE-DEFINE EACH COMPETENCY?
ACTING WITH INTEGRITY	
The ability to make decisions and take action through continual improvement of awareness and understanding; aligned with the organization's values and code of ethics.	
TALENT MANAGEMENT	
The ability to identify, attract, and develop the right person for the right role at the right time.	
UNDERSTANDING THE BUSINESS	
The willingness to stay abreast of emerging trends that may have a significant impact on the business or the organization.	
CUSTOMER SUPPORT	
The willingness to focus on helping customers with their concerns and providing them with value-added solutions.	
GATEKEEPING	
The willingness to help others participate in the process-project and stay on track.	
DISCOVERING	
The ability to ask credible and intelligent questions about the opportunities and demonstrating that he or she understands the issues from the customers' points of view.	

Consensus Competency Application: Exercise

What do you think of when you hear the terms "communication" or "social skills" or "flexibility"? How would you define each of the following? How would others define these same competencies? Make a copy of this exercise and ask others to identify what they think of when they hear these words. What is common to the people you asked?

COMPETENCY	PERSON #1	PERSON #2	PERSON #3
Communication			
Self-Regulation			
Social Skills			
Flexibility			
Diversity			

COMPETENCY	PERSON #1	PERSON #2	PERSON #3
Process			
Improvement			
Personal Integrity			
Empowerment			
Delegation			
Team Player			
Functional Acumen			

Notes:

Module Focus

Identifying core behaviors and practices; creating observable behaviors; writing to the rater; creating lead-in statements; creating single and dual rater response-scales; directional feedback; converting macro questions to micro questions; creating demographic questions; open-ended or free-text questions; importance rating questions.

PERSPECTIVES

DESIGNING IT

DEVELOPING IT

DEPLOYING IT

DELIVERING IT

Getting to Core Behaviors

You planned it. You designed it. You have a title. You have your competencies and have defined them. You completed the easy part. Now you need to develop your design into a viable behaviorally based assessment. Now you really need to get it good! Now you need to develop the items for each competency. The items you develop are the heart of your assessment. They represent what people do on the job. They are the details. Behaviors are performance based. They are more important than competency labels. They are the basis for self-directed action planning.

All too often developers stop after they have labeled their competencies. Yet it is critical to include those behaviors that measure each competency, based on your definitions. You need to give employees clues about what you mean by "vision" or "team building" or "communication," and that can be difficult. Your items will measure specific behaviors and practices. The greater your specificity, the easier it is for participants to create self-directed action plans.

You can only measure a person's communication skills (a competency) by identifying and assessing the behaviors that fall under the label "communication skills." Do you want folks to think generally or specifically? You can implement meaningful action plans only when you focus on the specific behaviors for each competency. Creating an action plan for problem solving is meaningless. What aspects of problem solving should participants build upon? Which aspects should participants develop? Your answer invariably identifies a specific behavior or practice.

Behaviors are more important than competency labels.

An item that reads "This person communicates effectively" says nothing. Create items that measure what you have decided are the core behaviors for "communicates effectively." Whenever possible, start your survey response options with a verb. For example, "To what extent does this person . . . "

> *a. Present information in an organized, logical manner*
> *b. Write in a style that you can easily understand*
> *c. Listen to you without interrupting*
> *d. Inform you about pending changes in work priorities*
> *e. Speak to groups of people with ease and confidence*

Let's assume that your assessment will include at least these competency labels: "communication," "delegation," and "ethics." How will you measure each competency? When you hear the word "communication," what do you see people do that is effective? How do effective people communicate with others—by speaking one-to-one, by speaking to groups of people, by writing memos, by e-mailing, by listening, by using hand gestures and facial expressions?

Everyone in any organization has to communicate with at least one other person. For example, managerial personnel need to communicate with those who report to them. Technical people need to communicate their ideas to those needing their expertise. Administrative personnel need to communicate with those they report to and to others within or outside the department. Salespeople need to communicate with their customers and internal personnel. How effectively people communicate often separates those who are successful from those who are not. And it is that behavioral effectiveness that you need to capture. It is that behavioral effectiveness that helps you separate observable behaviors from jargon and the latest HR-vendor fad *du jour!* Build upon your critical incidents and brainstorming results.

Measure Distinct Behaviors-Practices

Some developers group multiple kinds of items under a description. The separate items covered by that description will probably be taken as a whole by raters. Though to some folks, your assessment will appear short and quick to complete, this is not an effective format. You'll create confusion for the rater and the participant. Here are some examples of badly designed descriptions:

Dimension: Change Agent Leadership
- **Competency-Theme:** Consensus Building
  Description: Builds and collaborates among individuals and groups using consensus-building skills; summarizes opposing points of view; integrates opposing points of view; builds alternative solutions based on different points of view; displays courage when an issue is critical to the well-being of the organization's missions and values.

Option A: While each aspect of this description is distinct and separate in the mind of the developer, raters will read the description and respond to it as a whole. If you use this format, you'll create a dilemma for raters. What is the rater actually responding to in the above description? All descriptors, most, or some of the descriptors? Raters single out one or two aspects of the description and respond to the entire question accordingly. The problem for the participant is they do not know what raters were thinking when they responded to this description. What if raters indicated the participant was effective for this description? Does that mean effective with respect to all points included in that description? If the participant was identified as not effective, which points are weak — all, some, or just one? As a result, participants cannot be certain that they are effective or ineffective on this theme overall or with respect to just one or two areas within the description.

Some organizations use their mission and values as their model. If one value is expressed by something called "energy and change," include it in your assessment if you feel it is critical to the effectiveness of your employees. Some developers will include a list of descriptors for the value in question and use that as the actual item on their assessment. As with the previous example, this is not particularly useful, because this will present raters with multiple issues to respond to. As a result, participants (and you) never know which parts of that description or definition are strengths or weaknesses. For example, you may describe "energy and change" as when a person "has enormous energy and the ability to energize and invigorate others; sees change as an opportunity, not a threat." If the raters indicate the participant does this well (and so deserves a higher rating), did they mean that all descriptors for this value are effective? If the rating is low, did raters mean that all descriptors are ineffective or just the first part or just the second part? When ratings are high, participants will probably conclude they are effective across all descriptors. When raters are lower, they will become frustrated about which (if any) descriptors are strengths and which are weaknesses. This all amounts to some sloppy stuff!

Option B: You can choose to identify the theme-competency, then ask raters to select the most appropriate response for the participant they are assessing. Style-type assessments typically use this approach (as in a forced-choice format where raters select which adjective best describes this person, and so on). Some examples include the following:

1. Select the most appropriate descriptor of this person's ability to manage job stress:
   a. Often allows the normal stress in the job to block his/her performance.
   b. Usually handles stress without letting it impact performance.
   c. Is proactive and minimizes the job-related stress.
   d. Becomes hysterical and loses it.

2. Select the most appropriate descriptor of this person's knowledge regarding different applications for customer solutions:

    a. Has the basic understanding of our products' applications.

    b. Can describe the benefits and impact of product solutions to customers.

    c. Is considered an expert about all product applications and how they benefit customers.

    d. Is a sandwich short of a picnic.

3. Select the most appropriate descriptor of this person's process for penetrating key customer accounts:

    a. Contacts purchasing people who can influence buying decisions.

    b. Contacts decision makers directly.

    c. Builds consensus for favorable buying decisions by contacting purchasing people and key decision makers to understand how they intend to use our products and how they will impact their customers.

    d. Does not have a clue.

Raters would then select the descriptor that best describes the participant. That is, they would select "a" if they believed the participant "Has the basic understanding of our products' applications," or "d" if they believed the participant "Is a sandwich short of a picnic," and so on.

Option C: Take your description (re: options A and B) and break it down to its individual components-issues. The phrases that make up the description could serve as the behaviors and practices for your survey. Instead of raters reading the description as a whole, they would read it as having separate items. Raters would then respond to each item separately. For example, if your lead-in statement were "To what extent does this person . . ." or "How well does this person . . .," the raters could be asked to respond to each of the following:

1. Collaborate with you by using consensus-building skills, such as. . .?

2. Summarize different points of view in an objective manner?

3. Integrate differences of opinion to build alternative solutions to ongoing problems?

4. Create alternative solutions based on differing points of view (and so on)?

5. Handle stress without letting it impact performance?

6. Contact key decision makers directly to ....?

Which format should you use, option A, B, or C? Which format seems more relevant to you, the raters, and the participants?

Some Question Uglies

Write to what

you can observe.

You will find many well-written questions. You will also find some bad ones. Some people create survey questions that are meaningless: they do not measure much, they are too vague, and they confuse raters. Some questions focus on attitudes (which are not relevant to behavior assessment), some on personality (also not relevant), and some focus on observable behaviors and practices (very relevant). Your items need to answer the question *"What do I see the person doing on a day-to-day basis?"* not *"What I think the person does or what I have heard that person does."* You can assess and measure only what you observe.

Here are some real-world examples from different surveys and different authors. If these uglies work for you, have a party! If they help you think through what you really need to measure, great! If they help you write better observable items, better yet! If you are the author, the developer, well ... .

SOME QUESTION UGLIES	ASK YOURSELF THESE QUESTIONS AS A STARTING POINT
Has an engaging personality	What does "engaging" mean?
Asks you for advice	About what? What kind of advice? For what purpose?
Demonstrates effective communication techniques	What communication techniques are you talking about—listening, writing, speaking, non-verbal communication?
Is a good leader	What does "good" mean? What attributes would you use to define a good leader?
Generates new ideas	What kind of ideas? For what purpose?
Is a methodical problem solver	What does "methodical" mean? Thorough? Plodding? Analysis paralysis? How would you know someone is methodical? What do they do when they are methodical?
Is a hard worker	What does being a "hard worker" entail? What does this person do that makes you believe (s)he is a hard worker? What are the behaviors and practices?
Leads from the heart	This means this person is what? Emotional? Empathic? Shuns logic? Is a softy? How would you translate this into other languages so its meaning is clear?

SOME QUESTION UGLIES	ASK YOURSELF THESE QUESTIONS AS A STARTING POINT
Keeps me up-to-date	Keeps me up-to-date about what?
Is fast at responding	Responding to whom? Or about what?
Is close to the business	What does that mean? Lives in the neighborhood? Eats, sleeps, and thinks about the business 24/7?
Is a doer	A doer of what? What does the person do that makes you believe (s)he is a doer?
Is a nitpicker	"Nitpicker" is slang. What does someone do that makes you identify them as a nitpicker? Do they pick nits?
Is insecure	This is not a behavior or a practice, but a symptom of something. What behaviors make a person insecure? What do you see them do that makes them insecure? Or, what makes you identify them as insecure?
Is cloistered	Would you know what this means? Do they lock themselves away? Do they avoid people? Make this question more specific, more observable.
Has guts	Again, this is slang. Are you referring to internal body parts? Does this mean fortitude? Courage? Perseverance? Translate this into another language and see what you get!

SOME QUESTION UGLIES	ASK YOURSELF THESE QUESTIONS AS A STARTING POINT
Is curious	Curious about what? Curious about finding new ways of doing something? Curious about finding solutions to ongoing problems?
Is aware of triggers	Are these emotional triggers that could launch the person into ballistic mode? Is this a gun lobby or NRA thing?
Has presence	Huh?
Is resilient	To what? Stains, rust, disease, constructive criticism, adversity? To what and under what circumstances? Be more specific.
Behaves as an owner	Does this mean the person treats employees well? Is benevolent? Is a tyrant? Plays golf most of the day?
Delivers smoothly	Is this person a smooth talker? A smooth operator? What does this mean?
Is consistent	With respect to what?
Makes good decisions	Decisions about what? Under what conditions?

What you ask is what

you get.

Question Uglies Application: Exercise

Some items include multiple behaviors and practices. As I mentioned, this can be very confusing to raters. Do raters' responses imply that each behavior is a strength? Or do they mean that only some aspects are strengths? If so, which ones are strengths from a rater's point of view? When addressing action planning, participants will have similar confusions. They will experience frustration. What should they build upon? What should they develop? They cannot know from questions that include multiple behaviors.

Review the sample items on the following pages. What is the most appropriate competency or competencies based on the current wording of these sample items-questions? If necessary, how would you revise each item to reduce any confusion raters may experience?

SAMPLE ITEM-QUESTION	APPROPRIATE COMPETENCY	REVISIONS TO THE ITEM
Empowers and delegates by allocating decision-making authority and/or task responsibility to others.		
Is able to build effective teams and takes advantage of each team member's strengths.		
Assigns work based on available resources and time limitations, and provides fair and constructive feedback		
Uses appropriate interpersonal skills and communication methods to build constructive relationships.		
Assures that diverse needs are considered in hiring decisions and work assignments, and leverages the talents of each individual.		
Displays professionalism, ethics, integrity, and initiative.		
Applies financial principles and budgeting to ensure appropriate funding levels while monitoring expenditures.		
Integrates technology into the workplace efficiently and cost-effectively and in a timely manner.		

SAMPLE ITEM-QUESTION	APPROPRIATE COMPETENCY	REVISIONS TO THE ITEM
Applies high-level written communication skills to reports, memos, and other written documents and presents them in a clear manner in order to keep his/her audience engaged.		
Creates a sense of belonging and ownership among team members; is able to build effective teams and takes advantage of the different strengths of each individual team member.		
Applies the principles of change management to achieve stated organizational goals, and communicates those principles to others through his/her actions and words.		
Analyzes complex issues, absorbing a large amount of information quickly, and is able to prioritize what is important.		
Collates information and works backwards to clarify requirements and define training objectives.		
Able to handle stressful and adverse situations in a relaxed and patient manner without an undue show of emotion.		
Monitors satisfaction.		
Believes in him/herself.		

Thirty Red Flags

We all have our own writing styles. It is far easier to critique (aka criticize, slam, ridicule, or undercut) the writing of another person than to have that person critique your writing. People are funny that way. Nonetheless, there are several useful tips to consider when developing your items. Consider the following suggestions:

1. ***Use everyday language:*** *Remember the people who will be responding to your questions. Avoid internal jargon especially if you deploy your survey to external raters. Use language that is appropriate to the people who will complete your survey.*

2. ***Talk to the respondent:*** *Use the word "you" in your questions whenever possible. You are collecting information from one person at a time. You want each person's opinions and perspective. Talk to each of them directly.*

3. ***K.I.S.S:*** *Use short, simple, clear questions. Be clear and to the point. Keep it short and simple.*

4. ***Proof your work:*** *Avoid any grammatical or spelling errors. Proofread what you wrote. Then proof it again!*

5. ***Observe it:*** *Do not ask raters their opinion about what they have heard about another person or department. Ask them to rely on their observations.*

6. ***Forget attitudes:*** *Do not ask raters questions about someone's attitude. You can't see an attitude. You can't measure it. Actions are the result of our attitudes. Attitudes are not the result of our actions. Identify and ask about the action, the observable behavior.*

7. ***Measure actions:*** *What does someone do? What can you see them doing? What behaviors do you want to reinforce?*

8. ***Use action verbs:*** *Begin items with verbs. The verbs you choose identify the key behaviors you want raters to recall. Begin items with words such as "gives," "maintains," "writes," "listens," "guides," "helps," "creates," "presents," "provides," "approaches," "mentors," etc.*

9. ***Split infinitives:*** *Don't do it. Instead of "This person has the ability to clearly write," use "This person has the ability to write clearly." Instead of "This person has the ability to successfully achieve...," use "This person has the ability to achieve successfully . . ."*

Avoid jargon.

Use action verbs.

Avoid biased questions.

Be consistent.

10. **Avoid lengthy, complex questions:** *How long is long? You may believe that some long questions are justified. Then ask yourself, Why? Is the topic unfamiliar? Does it require a lot of explanation? When possible, write items that are between five and ten words long. If necessary, write two shorter questions rather than one long one.*

11. **Avoid biased or leading response questions:** *You can influence the results of a survey by how you word the question. For example, "How satisfied are you that you deliver timely responses when handling customer complaints?" A timely response by employees to a customer complaint is a positive response. Or, "How unprofessional is it when someone arrives late to a meeting?" You bias items with words like "unprofessional" and, therefore, the results.*

12. **Relate to the theme:** *Make certain the items you write relate directly to the theme or competency you want to measure.*

13. **Use consistent response scales:** *Keep your response scales to a minimum. You can confuse raters when you change your response scales for each question. If you begin your survey with a five-point response scale, continue to use a five-point scale as much as possible throughout your survey. If you want to change the scale anchors, do so, but keep the five-point scale. If you change the anchors and the scale points, do so with a block of questions or for an entirely new set of issues and themes.*

14. **Never reverse the value of the scale points:** *That is, if at first you identify a response of "1" as being low or ineffective on your scale and "5" as high, do not reverse the scale and suddenly make "1" high for a different set of questions and "5" a low response.*

15. **Use consistent wording:** *Keep your lead-in text for a set of questions the same. For example, "How satisfied are you that this person is . . . "*
    a. Responsive to your career development needs?
    b. Knowledgeable about our products and services?

16. **Avoid asking about more than one issue in the same question:** *Again, this is a very common error. Multiple issues or double-barreled issues result in confusing data. For example, "This person is polite and responsive and very professional when resolving retail and wholesale*

*complaints and delivery problems." If the rater ranks
the participant highly, does this mean the participant is
all of these things or only some of these things? Which
ones? Participants will not know which issues are the real
positive attributes and which are the negative ones
when they review their feedback elicited in this way.*

17. **Use commas, not "and" or "or":** *Using the word "and"
invites multiple issue questions. The word "and" connects
ALL the attributes you list before and after; the set needs
to be taken as a whole. When you use "or" you imply that
the rater must choose which attribute to provide feedback on (the words before or those after the word "or"),
as in "either-or." This means more confusion. Consider
using commas instead. Commas allow you to list separate
issues or attributes without linking each attribute or without
creating an "either-or" decision on the part of the rater.
Or better yet, create separate questions for each
attribute you want to measure, especially if they identify
two distinct attributes or behaviors.*

18. **He/she, she/he, they/them, us/our:** *When you include
all or many questions with her/him, he/she, they/them,
us/our you create longer questions for and boredom in
the respondent. Decide on a format, such as (s)he to
mean both he and she and stick with it as much as
possible throughout your survey.*

19. **Provide clear directions:** *Respondents need to know
what to do and how to complete your survey. Keep your
instructions simple and clearly written. If you want only
one response, write "Mark only one." If you want people
to respond to all that apply, write "Mark all that apply."*

20. **Reconsider using numbers:** *It can be difficult and time-
consuming for respondents to rank order items or to
include percentages as part of their responses. These
types of questions can be useful and they can cause
frustration (things may not add up to 100 percent or
some items may have equal weight to the respondent).
Decide which of the following items is easier for you to
respond to:*
    a. *Indicate the percentage of importance for each of
       the following six issues (must total 100%) . . .*
    b. *Identify if each of the following six issues are
       important to you (Yes, No, Somewhat)*

**Consider (s)he for she
and he.**

Avoid double negatives.

21. **Write behaviorally based questions:** *You may write questions such as "Shows discretion" or "Demonstrates leadership." Ask yourself, "What will this person be doing when showing discretion or leadership?" What does "discretion" mean? Does the person keep secrets? Is "Keeps confidential information confidential" better? How would you rephrase these examples?*
    a. *My favorite boss has a pleasing personality.*
    b. *Is asked by others for advice.*
    c. *Understands the importance of the difference between cause and effect.*
    d. *Knows how to use the advanced features of Chuckles software.*
    e. *Demonstrates effective techniques.*

22. **Minimize words such as "demonstrate" and "show":** *A behaviorally focused item describes how a person demonstrates a skill or competency. However, there will be times when you may not be able to describe a behavior that identifies a particular level of performance. In such cases, you may have to write, "To what extent does this person . . . Demonstrate an ability to present ideas in a persuasive manner." You can over-use words like "demonstrates" or "shows" or "illustrates." As much as possible, think through the behavior you want to measure, then frame your question. Ask yourself, "What does a person do when they demonstrate something, or show, or illustrate something?"*

23. **Avoid negatively worded items:** *Avoid using double negatives. You will see this construction in some psychological or style-type instruments. While the developer may not be confused about what (s)he means, the rater can become confused. Write items to focus on the behaviors you want to reinforce, that you want employees to do, not what you do not want them to do. Clear? How would you re-write these items?*
    a. *Shouldn't be inconsistent.*
    b. *Fails to listen to others.*
    c. *Does not dominate discussions.*
    d. *Does not believe that others are capable of doing good work.*
    e. *This person fails to tell people what not to do when assigning a task.*

    f. This person shouldn't be intolerant of others who do not show up on time for meetings.

    g. This person does not consistently perform up to expectations.

    h. Never generates negative outcomes.

    i. Does not see the need to discount irrelevant priorities when under time pressures.

24. **"Can you" or "will you":** Use the word "can" when you want to identify someone's ability to do something. Use the word "will" when you want to identify someone's motivation to do it. This is some fun psychology at work. If you ask someone if they will do something, they may say yes or no. Perhaps they have enough to do now and they will not (are not willing to) take on more work at this time. The word "can" implies ability or competency to do something. "Can you do this for me?" means do you have the knowledge, skills, and intellect to do this for me? Of course, a person might say, "Okay, I can do that for you!" but still say, "And I will not do it."

25. **Do not repeat your definition:** Avoid using the words from your definition of a theme in the response items as much as possible. For example, imagine your definition for "planning and goal setting" is "the ability to plan and organize work and set realistic measurable objectives for a work unit." If your lead-in text is "My favorite boss . . . ," your items could be:

    a. Plans and organizes work effectively.

    b. Sets realistic objectives for me.

    c. Sets measurable goals and objectives for our work unit.

26. **Avoid asking the same question twice:** Some people ask the same question, or a question that is very similar, in different sections of the survey. They do this to make sure the rater is responding honestly to the items. Don't do it. If raters believe you don't trust them, they will not trust you. Trust me! They will not. They may not complete your survey, or they may provide you with vanilla feedback—things they think you may want to hear and do not create conflict for the rater. They may always respond with a neutral "3" on a 5-point scale, for example.

"Can you" is different

from "will you."

Contrary to popular belief, there is no magic length to any instrument.

27. ***Do not stop at the theme-competency level:*** *"My favorite boss (or favorite team leader) has effective delegation skills." "This person communicates clearly." What do these questions mean? What constitutes delegation? What constitutes effective delegation? What does one do when one communicates? Are you talking about someone's speaking abilities, writing skills, listening skills, presentation skills, non-verbal behavior, or all of the above? When you can answer those questions, you have the items you need for your instrument.*

28. ***Include more than one or two items per competency:*** *You cannot measure any competency or theme with just a single item or two, though some would have you believe that. What few questions would you select to measure something called "Delegation" or "Problem Solving" or "Decision Making" or "Creativity" or "Integrity?" Include a sufficient number of items to measure each of them (re: content validity). If you cannot identify additional items, drop the competency.*

29. ***Play doctor-patient:*** *Get a second opinion. Have someone read your items and instructions. Have others read your assessment to identify any spelling or grammatical errors, any confusing directions, and any confusing or vague items.*

30. ***Think five items per competency:*** *Most folks want a short survey, but most end up with a survey longer than they initially expected. Some instruments are indeed short, consisting of less than fifteen items. Others are equal in length to some short-term careers, with over 150 items. The longer the instrument, the more information you collect. At some point, however, you need to analyze what you are doing. There is no magic length to any instrument. Write at least five items for each theme or competency. On average, a person can respond to six items per minute. So if you want to measure ten competencies, include at least five items per competency or fifty items. This means most respondents should complete the survey in about ten minutes or so. Can you include more than five items? Yes.*

Write to the "Yous" and "Yours"

Write your items so you are talking to the rater, the "you" (third person), in order to identify what the "I" (first person) has seen the participant do on the job. The purpose of 360-degree feedback is to obtain feedback about one person from multiple sources. Each source provides feedback based on his/her direct interaction with the participant. Each of these raters responds from her/his personal experiences with that participant. Write your items so raters can respond in terms of how "I observe" the participant, (but) not how "I heard" about what the participant does or does not do.

Many developers make the mistake (inadvertently or not) of writing items that focus on what a participant is believed to be doing or to have done rather than what the participant has been observed doing by a specific rater. Or assessments may include many items that certain raters cannot answer. Feedback from the immediate boss can be a case in point. The boss may not always know how well the participant motivates or delegates to a direct report. The sales manager may not always know what exactly the salesperson does or says during a sales call. As a result, the boss may respond based on what the boss thinks the participant is doing based on what others are saying. This, unfortunately, can occur more often than one would like to believe. The "you" and "your" in each of the following items refers to the rater, regardless whether that rater is the boss, customer, direct report, or peer. A rater who is identified as a peer to the participant responds accordingly. The response is from *that* peer's point of view. *That* peer does not respond as though (s)he were a boss or direct report. The 360-degree process relies on your feedback. You are focusing on observable behaviors. You want that feedback from each rater's perspective. Display the results by each rater group's perspective. The analysis includes identifying differences among each rater group.

Write your items in the third person to identify first-person observations.

Some Examples
To what extent does this person . . .
   Motivate *others* to work towards team goals and priorities?
   Call on *customers* on a regular basis?
   Handle *staff* concerns regarding project assignments to their satisfaction?
   Delegate tasks that build on *others'* strengths?

You-Your Examples
To what extent does this person . . .
   Motivate *you* to work towards team goals and priorities?
   Call on *you* on a regular basis?
   Handle *your* objections to *your* satisfaction?
   Delegate tasks that build on *your* strengths?

Participants do not generally delegate upwards to the boss. If there is no direct observation, the boss (or any other rater) should respond with a "Not Applicable." Unfortunately, many tend to respond to what they believe the participant does or what they have heard the participant does or what the participant probably does based on the boss's impression of that participant given his or her other behavior.

One option is to include a qualifier, such as "*others* plus *you-your*," or "*others* and a reference to a specific target population," so the item reads:

To what extent does this person . . .
   Motivate *you (or others)* to work towards team goals and priorities?
   Call on *you (customers)* on a regular basis?
   Delegate tasks that build on *your (or others')* strengths?
   Handle *your (customers')* objections to your satisfaction?

This option can allow you to cover a range of possibilities. This option works well as long as you do not include such qualifiers in the majority of your items.

Lead-In Text

I recommend you develop lead-in statements for the questions in your assessment. Do this before you write your items. Your lead-in text helps raters focus on the intent of your questions. Lead-in text can help you avoid repeating the same set of words over and over. Lead-in statements often end with ellipses or with colons. Your survey questions follow the lead-in.

There are many different examples of lead-in statements. Your lead-in statement is contingent upon your rating scale descriptors and vice versa, and it depends on what you want raters to think about as they respond to each question. Do you want them to think about *how effective* a person is with respect to the questions on your survey? Do you want them to focus on their *level of satisfaction* or *agreement* or how *frequently* they observe certain behaviors in the person they are assessing?

Typical lead-in statements:
How often does this person . . . (level of frequency)
To what extent does this person . . . (level of frequency)
To what extent do you agree that this person . . . (level of agreement)
How effectively does this person . . . (level of competency)
How satisfied are you with this person's performance in the following areas . . . (level of satisfaction)
How would you prioritize/rank the following . . . (degree of importance)

Your lead-in text and survey questions could be:
To what extent does this person (the person being evaluated) . . .
Cooperate with you to get the job done right the first time?
Keep you informed of critical decisions (s)he makes?
Willingly share critical information with you?
Listen to you without interrupting?
Identify performance expectations up front before you (or others) begin a task?

Your lead-in text for each question or a series of questions now makes grammatical sense for the questions you use in your survey. Should you choose not to include a lead-in statement, you'll need to repeat it for each question for the rater, which can get a bit tedious.

To what extent does this person cooperate with you to get the job done right the first time?
To what extent does this person keep you informed of critical decisions (s)he makes?
To what extent does this person willingly share critical information with you?
To what extent does this person listen to you without interrupting?
To what extent does this person identify performance expectations up front before you (or others) begin a task?

You are adding additional words to each sentence and are thus making your survey longer. As a result, raters will take longer to complete the survey. The repetition will cause people to become bored and impatient about completing the rest of the survey. As a result, your response return rate could be lower.

Rater Response Scales

Whenever you want quantitative feedback, you need to include some type of rater response scale. Quantitative feedback provides quantifiable feedback. The scale points typically are from 2 to 10. Most well-designed assessments use a Likert or BARS scale (Behaviorally Anchored Response Scale).

Once you establish the number of response points, you need to identify the response labels you want to use with your BARS. Each point on the scale should include a descriptor in the scale itself (e.g., 5=Always, 4=Almost Always, 3=Generally, 2=Almost Never, 1=Never). These descriptors help raters respond more easily to each item. Some vendors do not include descriptors for each point on their scale. This can be confusing to raters, and it is critical that raters understand the meaning of each scale point. BARS will help you accomplish that. By labeling each point, all raters understand the meaning of each point.

Some vendors use only numbers to identify the points on the scale (as in 1, 2, 3, 4, or 5). These are not Likert or BARS scales. A 2-point or dichotomous scale, such as "yes-no," is very simple. When you use this scale you clearly limit the range of responses. Nonetheless, depending on how you see the world and what you want to do with the data, a 2-point scale will provide you with applicable feedback.

Some people believe that 7-to-10 point scales will provide more discriminating information. A 10-point scale is nothing more than a doubling of a 5-point scale and most raters cannot (or choose not) to make such fine differentiations in their responses. If you believe your folks are a tad impatient, including a 10-point scale could create unhappy campers.

There is considerable debate whether respondents will actually take the time and make such discriminations. Researchers and academicians may do this. Highly analytical and statistical people may prefer such a scale, but experience shows that most people find it to be overkill and a bit of a bother. A 5-point scale provides a range of response options. It is simple. And it is sound from a psychometric perspective. Do you still prefer a 6-to-10 point scale? Then use it.

Odd or Even Scales

You will need to decide whether you want to use an odd or even response scale. Some researchers claim that when the response scale has an odd number of options, raters will tend to select the middle scale point. Raters, it is believed, will respond in the middle of the scale (and so exhibit central tendency) to avoid giving extreme feedback—whether overly positive or negative. This argument favors using the scales with an even number of response options. The issue of central tendency is a non-issue in my experience. Central tendency is more common in single-response scales than with dual-response scales. (It is very common in macro or employee opinion surveys, for example.) It is more a function of the rater's mindset as it relates to the process of giving feedback to a specific item in light of who or what they are evaluating. That is, if raters are not comfortable either with the process or with the person they are assessing, they may choose the midpoint to avoid any conflict. They may decide that providing feedback, albeit the vanilla variety, is safer for them. The underlying issues here are the rater's attitudes towards the 360-degree process in general, the participant they are assessing in particular, or the organization as a whole. *Do I trust them with my feedback? Will they identify my responses?* Conversely, if they are comfortable, most raters will not be bashful about identifying their *true* opinions. Will some items have an aggregate score that is on the middle of the scale (central tendency)? Yes. Will all or most display that tendency? No.

Even-numbered scales are forced-choice scales. Some raters may not want to respond if there is no neutral or mid-point on your scale. If there is no such midpoint, respondents often

Central tendency is more common in single-response scales than with dual-response scales.

(psychologically speaking) choose a more positive response, thus creating data that is positively skewed or slanted towards the positive. Raters may not appreciate being forced to respond one way or the other. You may have good reasons for including an even scale. The raters may have different reasons for responding to it. As a result, they may give you an answer that they believe you want to see. Or, they typically refuse to respond at all.

Consider including "not applicable" or "do not know" as a response point regardless of the number of points on the scale you choose. If you in essence want a 5-point scale, add another point, "not applicable," anyway. No one wins when raters close their eyes and make responses in order to get through the survey items. Many Web-based assessments require raters to complete all items before their data is compiled. I recommend that feature. Give raters a choice (an out) by including the "N/A" option. In this way, if they are bored, indifferent, nervous, suspicious about being identified, or just feel the item is not applicable to them, the "N/A" can provide a more honest response. And any compilation of the results should not include the "N/A" response as part of the tabulation of results.

The compiled feedback results should not include "not applicable" responses.

Multiple Response Scales

How many response scales will you use in your survey? Less is more. Some developers change rater response scales for each question. Other developers will change the response scale and the number of response points for each of those different scales. If you include too many scales, raters can become confused and may not realize that you have switched scales on them as they complete the survey. Keep it simple. It is best to group multiple questions or themes under the same response scale and with the same response points. For example, if you create a separate section called "Importance Ratings," list those competencies or issues that you want to include under this section. Your lead-in text may be something like, "How important are each of the following to you?" or, "Indicate how important it is for the person you are assessing to have each of the following when the two of you work together?"

Raters can then respond to all the competencies or issues listed under the same scale. For example, 1=Not as Important, 2=Somewhat Important, 3=Important, 4=Very Important, and 5=Extremely Important.

Other examples of your lead-in texts for an "Importance" section could be:

How important are each of the following items to you as you interact with this person:
How important are these items for this person's career development:
How important are these items for this person's current position-title:

Your competencies and their respective definitions follow your lead-in text:

Verbal and Written Communication: the ability to identify customer needs and expectations and to express a point of view or convey information effectively
Presentation Skills: the ability to organize and conduct effective presentations and demonstrations which focus on customer needs, expectations, requirements.
Personal Initiative: the willingness to demonstrate individual drive and responsibility for his or her actions

If you have to use multiple scales, group as many competencies and their respective behaviors-practices under the same scale. Then change scales and group the other themes under that new scale. There is no scale for the competency in this example, only for the items for that competency.

Competency: Presentation Skills
The five-point response scale for items listed under this competency is:
1=Not Very Effective; 2=Somewhat Effective; 3=Effective; 4=Very Effective; and 5=Highly (Extremely) Effective

If you want to measure importance for both the competency and each corresponding item, a single importance rating scale will suffice for both.

Competency: Presentation Skills

The five point response scale for this competency is:
1=Not Very Important; 2=Somewhat Important; 3=Important;
4=Very Important; and 5=Highly (Extremely) Important

Again, you can create multiple sections with different scales and include other competencies under them. Do not change response scales within a competency, and avoid having a different scale for each theme. Do not have one scale for a competency and a different scale for items listed immediately under that competency. This just generates confusion. Fewer scales mean less confusion.

5-Point Response Scales

Choosing a response scale for your survey is a key decision and will shape the type of information you collect from your employees or customers. It also affects how you write each question. What is the best number of response points to use in your survey? That depends; there is no one best answer. The best response scales have these basic attributes:

- Raters can easily understand them.
- They allow raters to discriminate between their points on the scale.
- They are easy to interpret.
- The data is easy to interpret from the scale.

Sample Scales to Get You Started

SCALES OF FREQUENCY	SCALES OF QUANTITY	SCALES OF QUALITY*
Almost Never	None	Poor
Sometimes	A Few	Fair
Generally	Many	Average
Frequently	Almost All	Good
Almost Always	All	Excellent
Never	Far Too Little	Much Lower
Seldom	Too Little	Slightly Lower
Occasionally	About Right	About the Same
Frequently	Too Much	Higher
Always	Far Too Much	Much Higher
Almost Never	Less than Two	Among the Worst
Occasionally	Two to Three	Less Well than Most
Often	Four to Five	Adequately
Usually	Six to Seven	Better than Most
Almost Always	More than Seven	Among the Best
		SCALES OF PERFORMANCE*
Rarely	Less than 2 Errors per Hour	One of the Worst
Sometimes	3-5 Errors per Hour	Below Average
Generally	6-8 Errors per Hour	Average
Frequently	9-11 Errors per Hour	Above Average
Almost Always	More than 12 Errors per Hour	One of the Best
SCALE OF EFFECTIVENESS	**SCALE OF INTEREST**	
Very Ineffective	No Interest	Very Low Performance
Somewhat Ineffective	Little Interest	Low Performance
Neither Effective nor Ineffective	Neutral	Moderate Performance
Reasonably Effective	Probably Interested	High Performance
Very Effective	Very Interested	Very High Performance
SCALE OF IMPORTANCE	**SCALES OF SATISFACTION**	**SCALE OF DEVELOPMENT**
Not (as) Important	Very Dissatisfied	Continuous Guidance Needed
Somewhat Important	Somewhat Dissatisfied	Frequent Guidance Needed
Important	Neither Dissatisfied nor Satisfied	Some Guidance Needed
Very Important	Somewhat Satisfied	Almost No Guidance Needed
Extremely Important	Very Satisfied	No Guidance Needed
SCALE OF AGREEMENT		**SCALE OF POTENTIAL**
Strongly Disagree	Not Satisfied	Very Little Potential
Disagree	Somewhat Satisfied	Some Potential
Neither Agree nor Disagree	Generally Satisfied	Average Potential
Agree	Very Satisfied	High Potential
Strongly Agree	Extremely Satisfied	Very High Potential

* Note: You can use a scale to measure different issues. For example, you can use a scale for quality to measure performance. Make certain your lead-in text and the wording of each item correspond to the response scale.

Scale Matrices

Response scales, such as those measuring frequency, can be combined with qualifiers and vice versa. You can incorporate the qualifier into your lead-in text statement. The following illustrates some lead-in text options for your response scales.

Lead-in text: How effectively does this person perform the following (practices):
Response scale: 1=Almost Never to 5=Almost Always

Lead-in text: To what extent does this person display exceptional performance in the following areas:
Response scale: 1=Almost Never to 5=Almost Always

Lead-in text: How often does this person take the initiative in the following areas:
Response scale: 1=Almost Never to 5=Almost Always

Lead-in text: To what extent is this person (prepared) or (competent) or (qualified) or (effective) in each of the following areas:
Response scale: 1=Almost Never to 5=Almost Always

Lead-in text: How often does this person (meet your performance standards) in each of the following (practices):
Response scale: 1=Almost Never to 5=Almost Always

Examples of a combined response scale could be:

1=Almost Never Qualified
5=Almost Always Qualified

1=Almost Never Prepared
5=Almost Always Prepared

1=Almost Never Collaborative
5=Almost Always Collaborative

1= Almost Never Meets Your Performance Expectations
5= Almost Always Meets Your Performance Expectations

RESPONSE SCALE: FREQUENCY QUALIFIER OPTIONS					
Almost Never	Qualified	Competent	Prepared	Effective	Exceptional Performance
Sometimes	Qualified	Competent	Prepared	Effective	Exceptional Performance
Generally	Qualified	Competent	Prepared	Effective	Exceptional Performance
Frequently	Qualified	Competent	Prepared	Effective	Exceptional Performance
Almost Always	Qualified	Competent	Prepared	Effective	Exceptional Performance
RESPONSE SCALE: FREQUENCY QUALIFIER OPTIONS					
Almost Never	Important	Team Player	Collaborative	Meets Your Performance Standards	Takes Initiative
Sometimes	Important	Team Player	Collaborative	Meets Your Performance Standards	Takes Initiative
Generally	Important	Team Player	Collaborative	Meets Your Performance Standards	Takes Initiative
Frequently	Important	Team Player	Collaborative	Meets Your Performance Standards	Takes Initiative
Almost Always	Important	Team Player	Collaborative	Meets Your Performance Standards	Takes Initiative
RESPONSE SCALE: QUALITY QUALIFIER OPTIONS					
Very Low	Performance	Potential	Ability	E-I*	Expertise
Low	Performance	Potential	Ability	E-I	Expertise
Moderate	Performance	Potential	Ability	E-I	Expertise
High	Performance	Potential	Ability	E-I	Expertise
Very High	Performance	Potential	Ability	E-I	Expertise

*Emotional Intelligence

Raters would respond to each behavior or practice based upon the lead-in text you use. For example,

(Lead-in text) How competent is this person in each of the following behaviors-practices:
    Take(s) the initiative to resolve ongoing problems

Or, (Lead-in text) To what extent is this person a team player when asked to:
    Adapt to new work procedures, standards

The feedback participants receive will be framed as:

(This person is) Almost Never competent to take the
initiative to resolve ongoing problems.
Or, (this person is) Almost Always competent to take the
initiative to resolve ongoing problems.

(Lead-in text) To what extent is this person a team player in
each of the following behaviors:

(This person is) Generally a team player when asked to adapt
to new work procedures, standards.
Or, (this person is) Almost Always a team player when asked
to adapt to new work procedures, standards.

Variations are wide ranging and depend on how you want to
measure what you want to measure. Here are some examples
of different lead-in statements and qualifiers along with
sample behaviors and practices. You could use a frequency,
quantity, or quality response scale, for example:

How qualified is this person to:
Serve as a subject-matter-expert to you.
Perform his/her work effectively in ambiguous,
changing situations.
Provide you with multiple solutions to ongoing problems, issues.

How competent is this person in the following practices-areas:
Applies effective win-win negotiation skills, such as . . . .
Assigns tasks to the most qualified person.
Challenges the status quo for how we get things done.

How prepared is this person in the following practices-areas:
Manages the allocation of human resources.
Provides pro-con arguments for her/his decisions.
Identifies alternative solutions when resolving problems.

How effective is this person in the following practices-areas:
Prepares a clear, understandable budget.
Knows what to delegate to whom based on that person's
proven abilities.
Adjusts his/her communication style to the situation.

How would you assess this person's potential in each of these areas:

Serves as a positive role model to you.

Motivates you to achieve the team's goals.

Perseveres in order to promote his or her ideas despite
peer pressures.

Takes risks appropriate to expected benefits, costs.

**How would you assess this person's ability in each of the
following behaviors-practices:**

Communicates ideas in a well-organized manner.

Summarizes key points to verify understanding.

Demonstrates patience when listening to you.

Raters can then respond to each item on a 5-point scale,
depending upon which scale you include in your assessment.

1=(This person is) almost never effective (with this behavior).

2=(This person is) occasionally effective.

3=(This person is) frequently effective.

4=(This person is) almost always effective.

5=(This person is) always effective (with this behavior).

1=(The participant's performance is) very low
(with respect to this behavior).

2=(The participant's performance is) low.

3=(The participant's performance is) average.

4=(The participant's performance is) high.

5=(The participant's performance is) very high.

(This person is)	(This person has)
1=Not Very Competent	1=Much Lower Potential
2=Somewhat Competent	2=Slightly Lower Potential
3=Generally Competent	3=Average Potential
4=Very Competent	4=Higher Potential
5=Exceptionally Competent	5=Very High Potential

(This person is)	(This person has)
1=Not Very Effective	1=No Ability
2=Somewhat Effective	2=Some Ability
3=Generally Effective	3=Average Ability
4=Frequently Effective	4=High Ability
5=Highly Effective	5=Exceptional Ability

Even-Response Scales

Okay, so let's say you prefer an even scale; you may be convinced that raters will select the middle point on an odd scale. Keep in mind that you can modify any odd-numbered response scale into an even-numbered scale (and vice versa, of course). Here are a few possibilities.

5-POINT SCALE	6-POINT SCALE	4-POINT SCALE	2-POINT SCALE
1=Strongly Disagree	1=Strongly Disagree	1=Strongly Disagree	1=Strongly Disagree
2=Disagree	2=Disagree	2=Disagree	2=Strongly Agree
3=Neither Agree nor Disagree	3=Slightly Disagree	3=Agree	
4=Agree	4=Slightly Agree	4=Strongly Agree	
5=Strongly Agree	5=Agree		
	6=Strongly Agree		
5-POINT SCALE	**6-POINT SCALE**	**4-POINT SCALE**	**2-POINT SCALE**
1=Never	1=Never	1=Never	1=(Almost) Never
2=Seldom	2=Almost Never	2=Occasionally	2=(Almost) Always
3=Occasionally	3=Occasionally	3=Frequently	
4=Frequently	4=Frequently	4=Always	
5=Always	5=Almost Always		
	6=Always		
5-POINT SCALE	**6-POINT SCALE**	**4-POINT SCALE**	**2-POINT SCALE**
1=Very Low	1=Very Low	1=Very Low	1=(Very) Low
2=Low	2=Low	2=Low	2=(Very) High
3=Acceptable	3=Sometimes Low	3=High	
4=High	4=Sometimes High	4=Very High	
5=Very High	5=High		
	6=Very High		
5-POINT SCALE	**6-POINT SCALE**	**4-POINT SCALE**	**2-POINT SCALE**
1=Not Important	1=Not Important	1=Not Important	1=Not (Very) Important
2=Somewhat Important	2=Not as Important	2=Somewhat Important	2=(Very) Important
3=Important	3=Somewhat Important	3=Very Important	
4=Very Important	4=Important	4=Extremely Important	
5=Extremely Important	5=Very Important		
	6=Extremely Important		

Incomplete Response Scales

As I mentioned, sometimes folks do not identify each of the scale points for the rater. Or they will identify two points as being relatively equal on the scale. This can happen with either odd or even response scales. This is a "you fill in the blanks" response scale. The developer will define the two end response points and the middle point, but not the remaining response points. My suggestion is to define each point on your scale. If you cannot or do not see the rationale for doing so, consider reducing the number of response points on the scale. If you cannot or do not identify each point on the scale, why bother having such a scale? If you think it is critical to expand your scale to 7, 8, 9, or 10 points, then label each point.

Here are some examples from 10-, 7-, 5-, and 3-point incomplete response scales:

1=The statement is true to a very small extent, never, or not at all.
2=(blank)
3= blank)
4=The statement is true to an average extent, about normal.
5=(blank)
6=(blank)
7=The statement is true to a very great extent, always, without fail.

1=To a very small extent, never, or not at all
2=(blank)
3=To an average extent, about normal
4=(blank)
5=To a very great extent, always, without fail

1=Fluent
2=(blank)
3=Not Fluent

Sometimes folks will combine two points on the scale. For example:

1-2=Not Important
3-4=Somewhat Important
5-6=Important
7-8=Very Important
9-10=Extremely Important

If you cannot or do not identify each point on the scale, why bother having such a scale?

1-2=Not Effective
3-4=Somewhat Effective
5-6=Generally Effective
7-8=Very Effective
9-10=Highly Effective

Combining points is not a good design practice. Reduce a combined 10-point scale to a 5-point scale; reduce a combined 8-point scale to a 4-point scale, for example.

A frequency scale and directional feedback identifies how satisfied raters are with the participant's *level* of behavior.

Frequency Response Scales

I prefer to measure a behavior's frequency, and have been doing so since 1976. There are benefits to using a frequency response scale. Typically, folks expect they and others should always do something better or should *almost always* do more of something. For example, if you were in sales and closed on a million dollars in sales last year and met your sales goals, it would be unlikely that your favorite boss would pat you on the head and tell you to back off and not sell as much this year. A participant may receive a low score (low = low frequency, such as "almost never," "sometimes," etc., in this example) on some aspect of problem solving. This would indicate the participant is not performing that aspect of problem solving effectively according to the raters. However, it could be that for that specific behavior the participant is not expected to perform at any higher level according to that rater group. You cannot know this with a single scale. With a dual-frequency scale, the participant could still receive a low score with respect to current performance and a low score with respect to expected performance. That is, the participant is rated as performing at a low frequency level, say "almost never," and is also *not expected to perform* at any higher frequency. The participant is not doing it now and is not expected to be doing it. This type of feedback is not a weakness, but in fact a strength. The participant is doing what is expected according to that rater group. There is less need for that behavior when the participant works with that rater group.

Single- or Dual-Response Scales

One of the critical areas many developers fail to consider is the output—what the data will look like and how participants will apply its results. If the output does not act as a catalyst for change, what is the point of your feedback process?

Single-scale assessments are the most common and typically focus on current behavior only. Both single-scale and dual-scale assessments can identify how frequently a person performs a behavior or practice; how satisfied raters are with the participant as (s)he performs that behavior; how important behaviors and competencies are to rater groups; how effective participants are with those behaviors and practices, and so on. Single-scale assessments cannot measure both current and expected performance. Only a dual-scale assessment can do that. Single-scale assessments typically do not identify a direction for implementing needed change, which is an essential component when participants create self-directed action plans. Single-scale assessments can cause participants to misunderstand the consequences of their behavior as they interact with others.

Single-scale surveys do not provide participants with directional feedback.

Dual-scale assessments that focus on comparing current behavior with expected behavior are different, and provide participants with greater insights regarding the consequences of their actions. They include a direction for implementing needed change and, as a result, help participants create more relevant action plans. When you present the feedback results to participants in a horizontal bar graphic, for example, the dual-response scale format allows participants to visualize the delta or gap for each item within *and* among each rater group. Single-response scales cannot do this.

You can easily integrate a frequency response scale with a dual-scale assessment in order to provide participants with directional feedback and facilitate their action-planning efforts. The behavioral anchors for both scales are the same. For example:

The lead-in text could be: *How often does this manager . . .*
The behavior could be: Serve as a resource person on whom you rely for technical/professional advice?

The current response scale could be (How often does this occur?):
   1=Very Infrequently, 2=Once in a While, 3=Sometimes;
   4=Fairly Often; 5=Very Frequently
The expected response scale could be (How often should this occur?):
   1=Very Infrequently, 2=Once in a While, 3=Sometimes;
   4=Fairly Often; 5=Very Frequently

The report output graphically displays the difference or gap (if any) between current and expected performance. The greater the gap between what a participant does and what raters think (s)he should do, the less satisfied raters are with that performance. Conversely, the closer the gap, the more satisfied raters are with the participant's performance. The direction indicated by the graphic identifies what the participant or a group of participants could *do more of* or *less of*. This can also help trainers, coaches, and mentors identify what topics and issues to focus on in training programs or in one-to-one coaching and mentoring sessions.

Gene W. Dalton and William G. Dyer introduced the dual-response scale in 1973.

I became familiar with the concept of gap analysis while at 3M in 1972, before I knew about the label. As part of my training needs analysis process for any 3M client, I first listened to what key division managers described as the behaviors of effective sales and sales management people. I made calls with their salespeople and observed and recorded what they actually did. I then compared my observations to what I was told they were supposed to do. The greater the delta or difference (the gap) between current and expected behavior, the less effective was that individual or group of individuals. I then recommended and included those behaviors and practices into my 3M sales training program(s).

I first came across the phrase "dual-response scale" in writing in a survey titled, "Organizational Improvement Survey," developed by Gene W. Dalton and William G. Dyer, in 1973. Their survey included a dual-response scale that focused on frequency and importance. My focus since 1976 has been on a frequency of performance dual scale. One scale measures current-state observable behavior. The second scale measures expected future-state behavior.

Gap Analysis

These are two very popular words when folks talk about developing people. Most assessment providers talk about gap analysis as it relates to their single-scale assessment. There is gap analysis and True Gap Analysis.™ True Gap Analysis™ provides directional feedback for participants and requires a dual-response scale. You can discuss gap analysis from at least two points of view. There is *inter-rater* gap analysis and *intra-rater* gap analysis.

Inter-rater gap analysis: This is the most common use of gap analysis. It compares data from the participant with that from the other rater groups, such as the favorite boss, staff, peers, and customers. Just about every 360-degree assessment software program allows you to do this. Both single- and dual-scale assessments provide this type of gap analysis.

Intra-rater gap analysis: *True Gap Analysis™* identifies differences within each rater group. This type of gap analysis allows participants to see inside their data for each rater group and among all rater groups. That is, participants can identify the number of direct reports who have identified a difference, or gap, between how they assess the effectiveness of the participant and how that same participant assessed their own effectiveness. They can also see how many raters had the same assessment as the participant. Participants quickly realize that not all of their direct reports, for example, have the same expectations. They realize that not all direct reports are equal; what they expect from the participant can be different.

Just as this type of analysis allows participants to look inside their data, it also gets them thinking about who is inside their department. People are different. People have different styles. We may all be equal from a social or legal perspective, but not from a genetic or emotional perspective. Folks have different opinions of who is effective and which behaviors are effective and which are not. There is no one best way for a manager to manage all of the folks who report to him/her. Intra-rater gap analysis allows participants to develop more specific developmental action plans. Intra-rater gap analysis also allows participants to compare inter-rater differences.

True Gap Analysis™ provides participants with directional feedback and can act as a catalyst for implementing needed change.

Participants can compare and discover differences between their views and those of the boss, peers (inter), and within the peer rater group itself (intra).

The specificity of intra-analysis allows participants to identify how they may need to modify their behavior, for example become more flexible, as they interact with their peers or direct reports or customers or team members. Dual-scale assessments, coupled with response distributions, allow participants to identify how many in each rater group want them to change and in what direction they want them to change. Is it one direct report out of five who wants change? Or is it four out of five? It can also identify whether there is rater inconsistency within a rater group. For example, do some direct reports observe the participant as highly effective while at the same time another rater sees that person as highly ineffective? Perhaps a third or fourth rater sees that person somewhere in between. All data is presented. Olympic scoring is irrelevant here (or anywhere in my opinion). This delta or gap tells the participant that people within that group have different expectations. Not all direct reports agree as to the participant's effectiveness with this behavior.

Knowing this will affect action planning. It can mean that a sufficient number of direct reports recommend the participant change his/her behavior, either by *doing more* or *doing less* of that behavior. On the other hand, the data can mean that while not all direct reports are perfectly satisfied, enough are satisfied such that perhaps a developmental action plan is not necessary for that specific behavior.

What a participant says about him/herself in a performance-based 360-degree assessment is important. What others say about him/her is more important. The gap or discrepancy between a person's assessment and the assessments of other raters and other rater groups is the most revealing and meaningful information a person can gain from the 360-degree feedback process. The greater the alignment between a participant's behavior and the expectations of others, the greater that person's effectiveness and influence with them. The greater the discrepancy, the less effective and influential the person is. Gap analysis among and within rater groups provide more specific feedback to the participant. It

Directional feedback is feedforward. It identifies the direction participants need to change to become more effective—do more, do less, clarify before changing, build on strengths.

collaborates strengths and areas of weakness. It can identify blind spots. It can identify areas of hidden strength that the participant was not aware of. It can also identify discrepancies where the participant's behavior is ineffective and not productive.

Directional feedback is real world. It mirrors what organizations do day in and day out. At the start of the fiscal or calendar year, folks within organizations identify where they are and where they intend to be (or at least where they hope to be) by the end of the year or some other specified time period. The greater the distance between current and expected behavior, the more effort needs to be expended to reach that goal. Organizations then determine the right direction to reach their goal. Performance-based intra-rater gap analysis is the same.

Behavior Change

- In order for participants to improve, they first need to know where they are now (current behavior).
- They need to identify where they want to be or need to be (expectations).
- They need to identify action steps to get them there.
- They need to hold themselves responsible for their development, follow-up actions, and progress.
- They need to measure their progress towards their action plans and goals, and make any needed corrections.

The fundamental rationale for 360-degree feedback is to gather feedback from others.

Do not expect different results from the same behavior.

Revising Items Application: Exercise

Just for fun, here are some sample questions you could use to create your own surveys. Use them as they are. Review, select, and revise any items to your style of writing (keeping in mind the "Thirty Red Flags"). Write your questions to match your lead-in text and rating scale. Integrate what you have learned to complete this exercise.

Your lead-in text is: _____

Your rating scale is: _____

Your qualifier (optional) is: _____

EXISTING ITEMS	YOUR REVISIONS-MODIFICATIONS
My favorite boss provides me with the training to do my job effectively.	
Is easy to talk with.	
Willing shares the information I need to do my job more effectively.	
My manager supports the decisions I make.	
Our team leader promptly confronts poor performance.	
My supervisor deals with conflict before it gets out of hand.	
Creates a clear comprehensive vision of the future often the distant future.	
Manages through uncertainty by weighing up the options and evaluating tactical and strategic risks.	
Develops meaningful relationships and sharing processes within the organization.	
Thinks laterally to see ways around constraints and processes.	
Where appropriate, supplements own capabilities by soliciting views and obtaining information from others.	
Communicates necessary information and coordinates with appropriate people on projects and issues and seeks input from others while listening carefully to what others have to say.	
Gets it done.	

EXISTING ITEMS	YOUR REVISIONS-MODIFICATIONS
Upper management makes the tough, practical decisions.	
Consistently performs high quality work.	
Encourages people to voice their opinions.	
Sets high performance standards.	
Provides clear short- and long-term plans.	
Pays attention to those details that are critical to me.	
Shares relevant information with me so I can do my job more effectively.	
Shares information in a timely manner with other teams and functions.	
Provides constructive feedback in a timely manner.	
Presents ideas in a well-organized manner.	
Follows through with clearly written memos, correspondence.	
Keeps me up-to-date on changing priorities, budget constraints, time lines.	
Conducts meetings effectively by setting agendas, distributing the agendas ahead of time, keeping meetings on track, and following up with others on decisions agreed to.	
Anticipates potential resistance to solutions to problems.	
Understands the customers' business operations, issues, trends, opportunities.	
Compares the benefits of our products with those from the competition.	
Identifies opportunities to develop new products and services from existing products and services.	
Deals with crisis.	
Enjoys an empowering culture and participative management style that facilitates self-accountability and a sense of ownership.	
Negotiates.	
Does not alienate people.	
Pays attention.	
Does not criticize me for not doing what is not expected of me.	
Understands where people are coming from.	

Converting Macro to Micro

Suppose you have an employee opinion survey, or an organizational climate survey, or a training needs analysis survey, or a customer satisfaction survey. Could you convert the items from these macro surveys into a micro survey like a 360-degree assessment? Yes and no. It depends on the themes you have in those surveys. If the focus is on benefits, policies, and procedures, then the answer is no. If the themes focus on issues related to the effectiveness of people; employees' opinions of management, their department, or team; and deliverables such as customer service or technical support, for example — then the answer is yes. In fact, the conversion is easy.

Macro instruments report data by demographics, i.e., by managers or by supervisors or by team or by function or other demographic grouping. With slight changes to the wording of your questions and lead-in statements, you can identify, for example, the level of effectiveness for a specific manager's delegation effectiveness. You can easily transform a macro survey into a micro survey and vice versa. For example, if one item on your employee opinion survey (macro) asks employees to "Identify how effectively managers delegate in your department," you can modify this item to focus on the effectiveness of a specific employee (micro). Ask, "How effectively does your immediate manager delegate to you (or others)?" Here are a few more examples to consider.

THE WORDING IN YOUR MACRO SURVEY IS:	YOUR REVISED WORDING FOR A MICRO SURVEY IS:
MY SUPERVISOR:	TO WHAT EXTENT DOES THIS PERSON:
• Keeps me informed about what is going on in the organization.	• Keep me informed about what is going on in the organization.
• Sets a personal example of excellent customer service.	• Set a personal example of excellent customer service.
• Gives us a clear picture of the direction in which we are going.	• Provide me with a clear picture of the direction in which we are going.
• Encourages innovation and risk taking.	•Encourage me (others) to be innovative and take risks.
• Shows commitment to quality by funding improvement programs, seminars, and in-house training.	•Reinforce a commitment to quality by funding improvement programs, seminars, and in-house training.

Conversion Application: Exercise:

Here are some examples from macro surveys. How would you revise them for your 360-degree assessment?

Your lead-in text is: _____

_____

_____

THE WORDING IN YOUR MACRO SURVEY IS:	YOUR REVISED WORDING FOR A MICRO SURVEY IS:
• My supervisor treats all employees equally and fairly and does not show "favoritism."	
• New ideas are encouraged by the management in my department.	
• Changes in work priorities are communicated clearly to employees in my department.	
• Our benefits and opportunities for promotion are competitive with similar organizations.	
•My company is effective at eliminating unnecessary meetings and paperwork.	
• Management sees change as an opportunity rather than a threat.	
• The work I do is meaningful and challenging to me.	
• I am able to make decisions and resolve problems without checking with my immediate supervisor.	

Demographic Questions

These are optional. You collect demographic information on the participant in a 360-degree instrument (in contrast to an employee opinion survey, where you collect this information on all those who responded to the survey). Demographic items require a multiple-choice response format. Think of them as forced-choice questions where only one response is required per demographic item. You are asking "Who are you?" questions. You compile and present demographic data on groups of participants, not on any one individual participant.

I recommend that you include demographic questions in your instrument. This will facilitate comparing different groups when you are ready to analyze your data. The data can help you identify which demographic is more effective than another and which needs specific training programs, and so on. Include those questions that will give you the basic information you need to analyze the results. Do not include any questions about demographics if the total number of participants for that group is less than five. Presenting data with a small n-demographic invites folks to guess which participant is the least effective compared to the others. With a small number of responses, the data may not provide you with any meaningful conclusions.

You can include as many questions about demographics as you want. However, the more demographics you include and the more choices you include for each demographic, the more likely you will create paranoia among your employees. They will become nervous about being identified. Include only those demographic items that will give you information that you want and need. If you do not care about comparing the responses of men to women, for example, then do not include a demographic about gender.

You need to provide choices for each demographic. For example, if you ask, "What is your current title?" you could get a wide range of responses. Guide the rater. Include the title or position choices relevant to your organization (e.g., supervisor, team leader, manager, executive, general slacker). Your choices allow you to easily aggregate the data by all those participants who said they are managers who indicated they are located in Biloxi and/or who have been with the organization for five to eight years. This will allow you to compare the relative effectiveness for participants under each demographic choice. Some typical (and perhaps not so typical) demographic questions are shown on the following page. Again, include demographic choices that apply to your organization.

DEMOGRAPHIC QUESTION	DEMOGRAPHIC CHOICES
What is your gender?	Female
	Male
	Who wants to know
How many cross-functional moves have you had since joining the organization?	Only 1
	2-3
	4-5
	6-7
	Too Many
Which best describes your current function?	Administration
	Communications
	Customer Service
	Engineering
	Human Resources
	Manufacturing
	Quality Assurance
	Sales
	Voice of Reason
In which office (location) do you work?	Basseterre
	Bucharest
	Calgary
	London
	Minneapolis
	New York
	Singapore
	Way Out There
What is your current title?	Individual Contributor
	Supervisor
	Manager
	Executive
	The Big Boss
How long have you held your current title?	0-2 Years
	3-4 Years
	5-8 Years
	9-12 Years
	Too Long
What is your current status?	Full-Time Employee
	Part-Time Employee
	Independently Wealthy
	Overworked
	Underpaid
How long have you worked for this organization?	0-2 Years
	3-4 Years
	5-8 Years
	9-12 Years
	Like, Way Too Long

Once you have captured the data, you can create demographic reports manually or automatically through your software. Your software should allow you to click on the demographic question you want to analyze. For example, you may want to identify the relative strengths and weaknesses of women managers in general. You would select "Women" under the demographic titled "Gender." Simple. Or you may want to identify the strengths and weaknesses of women managers ("Gender") who have been with your organization for five years or longer ("Years of service") and who are located in your Midwest facility ("Location"). You can do this as long as you create demographic questions that will give you what you need for the comparative analyses you want and need later on. If you do not create the appropriate demographic items with their relevant options, you will be doing more manual tabulations than you may want to do later on.

Open-Ended Questions

Qualitative feedback can support and reinforce quantitative feedback.

Qualitative feedback can provide you (and participants) with a well-rounded feedback profile. Qualitative feedback does not include a rating scale or numbers or a score. Open-ended or free-text comments allow raters to express their opinions in as much detail as they want. Their comments typically go beyond what you have included in your survey and, as a result, can provide some valuable insights. You can include this type of feedback in at least three locations on your 360-degree assessment survey.

Option One: Include a comment box for each item or selected items. Each item on your survey includes a rater response scale (quantitative data) along with a comment box where raters can include any additional comments they want for that specific question. Such comments can provide participants with more insights. This will add to the length of your survey, however.

Option Two: Include open-ended questions for each theme-competency or selected themes-competencies, rather than for each question.

Option Three: Include a set of free-text questions at the end of your survey. These items are not necessarily linked to any one theme or competency, but are stand-alone items. Raters can complete these questions or not. Comments are automatically linked and grouped by the open-ended question. To remain anonymous, they typically are not linked to any rater group.

You can include as many open-ended comments as you like in your 360-degree assessment. In fact, you can create a 360-degree assessment with just open-ended comments. You can combine your qualitative questions with quantitative questions for any of these applications. With a 360-degree survey, consider at least these open-ended (or free-text) questions:

START DOING	What could this person start doing to work more effectively with you?
STOP DOING	What could this person stop doing to work more effectively with you?
CONTINUE DOING	What could this person continue doing?
OTHER QUESTIONS TO CONSIDER	What other comments would you like to share with this person? What two training programs would you recommend to this person? What could this person do to work more effectively with you? Identify this person's top three strengths when working with you. What is the one quality you especially like about this person? What one training program would benefit this person the most?

Importance Ratings

Importance ratings are often given their own section in 360-degree assessments. Some developers include an importance rating for each competency. Importance ratings, in general, can be useful because they help set priorities for self-directed change and improvement; they help identify differences among the participant and their rater groups. For example, what if the participant and the favorite boss indicated that handling customer objections and account penetration were high priority and the customers (internal or external) indicated that both these areas were low priority? Perhaps customers indicated that personal integrity and follow-through were high priority. Whose rating is correct? Whose rating should the participant pay attention to? In such instances, participants are between a rock and a hard place. Do they ignore what customers view as important? Or do they go the political route and go with their favorite boss's ratings? At the very least, any differences are a topic for discussion between the immediate manager and the participant.

Importance ratings can identify the "real" culture within your organization.

Importance Ratings for Competencies

Importance ratings for each competency can be beneficial. When you roll up participants' data to create a group profile, the aggregated data can identify organizational development issues. If upper management touts quality as their number-one priority and has festooned the halls and buildings with signs claiming customer satisfaction is number one, only to discover that the folks on the factory floor have rated it as "Who cares?" —then the organization may have a problem. Management can put up more banners, of course. They could also ask:

- Why don't our employees see customer satisfaction as a priority?
- Why do they think as they do about this issue?
- What are we (management) doing that does not reinforce the quality we value?

Importance Ratings: Some Examples

Directions: As you think about the person who asked you to complete this survey, ask yourself, "Which skills are more important for this person to have when the two of you interact together?" Distinguish the more important skills from those of lesser importance. **_Note:_** If you are the participant, indicate how important it is for you to have each of these skills.

Lead-in text: Indicate how important it is for the person who asked you to complete this survey to have each of the following competencies when the two of you interact together . . . .

Response Scale: Not as Important=1, Somewhat Important=2, Important=3, Very Important=4, Extremely Important=5

1. **Initiative and Risk Taking:** The ability to demonstrate individual drive and accept responsibility for his/her actions.
2. **Personal Integrity:** The ability to gain the trust and confidence of others by interacting in a fair and honest manner.
3. **Vision:** The ability to create and describe an ideal state or condition and align others toward its accomplishment.
4. **Quality of Results:** The commitment to produce high quality work (research, procedures, services, products) consistently, over time.

Importance Ratings for Behaviors

You may want to assess the importance of each behavior. But bear in mind that doing so could be overkill and greatly increase the length of your assessment. If you can, keep importance ratings to macro issues, such as competencies, rather than have raters rank each individual item in terms of importance.

You may want to use importance in a dual-scaled item set. This can work, but it may not be as practical as you hope. You could create dual-scale items that measure current behavior and how important that behavior is to the rater, participant, or the work unit. The delta, or gap, will be the difference between what raters observe and the importance they give to what they are assessing. The focus then tends to shift from

Test it before you rest it!

a behavioral issue to an importance issue. What you will get is not directional feedback (though, of course, you may not care about that). If the data indicates that the participant almost never does this behavior but raters see the behavior as very important, should the participant consider increasing that behavior to reflect the level of importance? Or, if the participant always does some behavior, but its importance rating is low, should the participant do less of that behavior? On the other hand, if the data indicates that the participant almost never does a behavior but is expected to, perhaps the participant should at least consider doing more of that behavior. My suggestion is that you keep a dual-scale consistent with what you want to measure. Include a separate importance ratings section and keep it at the competency level rather than the behavior-practice level.

Beta-Test Before Deployment

You are done! You've developed your assessment and now you can unleash it. Not so fast. Beta-test it first. Conduct a pilot run. Identify people within your own department or corner of the world who can evaluate your work. Tell them that their goal is to identify any confusing instructions or questions. You'll want to know, for example, whether they can access your Web-based survey, exit and enter it as often as they want, and save their responses as they do. You'll want them to respond to each question so you can then print out a sample profile to see what the data looks like in the reporting formats.

Store your ego during this process. Drop any items that are not relevant. Revise any items that are fuzzy or confusing. Refine your instructions if necessary. Make whatever changes your beta-test folks suggest. Then beta-test again to make certain everything is the way it should be. When all is well, unleash it.

Your programmers already know about beta testing. If you have built your own software, you may want raters to respond to specific items in a very specific way. In this way, you can check the logic of your software to make certain the data is correct. That is, if 100 raters completed and returned their survey, do you see the data for all 100 raters? If a specific number of raters responded to a specific question with "N/A," is that indicated in the "valid n" data compared to the "total n" data? If you have created a dual-response scale assessment, you will want to verify the ways you present directional feedback—do more, do less, build on strengths, and clarify. You can do this by creating a simple matrix with the number of the item and how you want each rater in each rater group to respond to that item. You can create items with large and smaller gaps. Then when you compile the data you can easily check the appropriate report(s) to make certain those items that should have a certain gap size have, in fact, that gap size, and so on.

Notes:

Module Focus

Randomizing your questions; ensuring success when you deploy your survey; increasing rater response ratios; rater bias; bribing raters; preventing apathy and boredom.

PERSPECTIVES

DESIGNING IT

DEVELOPING IT

DEPLOYING IT

DELIVERING IT

How to Ensure Success (Initially)

Maybe your assessment looks great on paper (and perhaps even greater in your mind). Maybe everyone even buys into it. Sounds like you're ready to unleash it. What can you do to help your feedback project roll out with fewer problems and political barriers? Here are some suggestions to get you started.

Randomization of Items

You've developed your items. You beta-tested your Web-based assessment. All has been blessed and approved. You are ready to deploy. How will raters see each item? Do you want all raters to respond to items in the same order? You can decide whether you want to group items under their appropriate theme or competency heading, such as "Communicating," "Problem Solving," "Delegating," "Empowering," and so on. Or you can list items in the same sequence without also listing the competency heading. Or you can randomize your items without the competency heading.

Randomization is appropriate to 360-degree assessments: it can minimize bias; it can minimize the Halo, Horns, and Pygmalion effects; and it can prevent raters from comparing their responses before they submit them. In short, it prevents collusion (which is one fear people have about 360-degree assessments). The concept of randomization allows you to change the sequence of items for each rater, automatically, whenever you deploy your assessment or whenever a rater logs into your Web-based assessment. Your software should do this for you. Once all raters have completed and submitted and locked their responses, your software should automatically reconfigure the sequence of items into a pre-determined order. As a result, when you are ready to transmit or print the feedback results, all participants see all competencies and their respective items in the exact same sequence. There are at least three randomization options available to you: no (none), intra-, and inter-randomization.

Randomizing items within your Web-based 360-degree assessment can prevent raters from colluding with one another.

No Randomization: Survey items always appear in the same order for all raters. If you have included themes or competencies in the body of your assessment, all items appropriate to that theme or competency will appear in the same numeric order, as will each theme. For example, the first theme ("Communication") will always appear first, followed by the five to ten questions for that theme. All raters respond to these items in the same order. When you produce the results, all participants will see their data in this same sequence, for example, by competency:

SURVEY SEQUENCE	RESULTS SEQUENCE
Item One	Item One
Item Two	Item Two
Item Three	Item Three
Item Four (and so on)	Item Four (and so on)

Intra-Randomization: You can change the sequence of each item within a theme or competency set. The first theme, "Communication," will always appear first: however the numeric sequence of the five to ten items will change whenever any rater logs on. If ten raters were to log on simultaneously, each would see a different item as the first. When you compile the results, all participants would see their data in the same sequence as all other participants. This is handy because it will not confuse the facilitator, nor will it confuse the participants if you conduct a group workshop to discuss the feedback results. The sequence of items for each rater could be something as follows, yet the sequence of the results is the same for all raters.

SEQUENCE OF YOUR COMMUNICATION ITEMS:			
RATER 1 SURVEY	RATER 2 SURVEY	RATER 3 SURVEY	COMPILED RESULTS FOR ALL RATERS
1	5	4	1
3	2	5	2
5	3	2	3
4	1	3	4
2	4	1	5

Inter-Randomization: You do not identify the theme or competency. Instead, all items are automatically randomized whenever a rater logs on to complete the survey. No theme heading is listed. Even when two raters log on at the same time, the item listed as the first for one rater will be different than the first for the second rater. This method helps ensure that raters are responding to each behavior separately, rather than responding to a set of behaviors (under the theme heading "Communication"). Collusion is almost impossible. As with intra-randomization, when you compile and produce the results all raters will see the same first item due to the magic of your software program.

SEQUENCE OF COMPETENCY-ITEM WHEN RATERS LOG ON:			SEQUENCE OF RESULTS:
RATER 1	**RATER 2**	**RATER 3**	**ALL RATERS**
IPC: 5	PI: 41	M: 29	IPC: 1
D: 12	PI: 42	D: 13	IPC: 2
PI: 40	PS: 19	IPC: 3	IPC: 3
M: 32	D: 11	PI: 43	IPC: 4
PI: 40	M: 30	M: 33	IPC: 5
And so on ...	And so on ...	And so on ...	And so on ...

Note: IPC=Interpersonal Communication Skills (items 1-8); D=Delegation (items 9-16); PS=Problem Solving (items 17-23); M=Motivation (items 29-35); and PI=Personal Integrity (items 36-43)

Manual Randomization

First, some history. Prior to 1990, vendors relied primarily on a paper format to collect 360 data. As a general practice, every 360 assessment we developed incorporated the inter-randomization format. Initially, we intended to purchase software that would help us randomize items. A programmer offered to create a table for us to facilitate this process, so we wouldn't have to purchase additional software. Our systems analyst (bless her heart!) said we could save time and money using a telephone book. Say what? Purists may take issue, but this is a proven method to randomize your items. We used this method from 1976 to 1999 with great success. Here is how we did it and how you can do it.

List the number of quantitative items in your assessment in numeric order. Do not include any demographic or open-ended comments.

Use your local telephone book (white pages) and open it (randomly) to any page.

If your assessment includes 100+ items, use the last three digits of the phone numbers on the page you just opened. If your assessment includes less than 100 items, use the last two digits from each phone number as your starting point.

If your assessment includes 1000 items or more (whew!), use the last four digits.

Assume that you have an assessment with 99 items. Randomly select a phone number. If the first phone number you choose ends in 37, that number (37) becomes the random placement of item (1) on your assessment. That is, raters would see your first item as item (37). If the next phone number ends in 2463, then raters would see the second item as item (63) in the sequence, and so on.

Cross off each item on your assessment as you assign its randomized order. Continue the process until you have randomized all 99 items.

ITEMS IN YOUR MASTER LIST	LAST DIGITS OF PHONE NUMBER	ITEM SEQUENCE ON YOUR PRINTED SURVEY
One (01)	9955	55
Two (02)	8820	20
Three (03)	9898	98
Four (04)	2221	21
Five (05)	0045	45

In this example, Item One (01) on your master list of items becomes Item Fifty-five (55) on your printed survey; Item Two (02) becomes Item Twenty (20), and so on.

Recommended E-mail Messages

Develop a Pre-deployment message. Send an e-mail message within one week of your actual deployment date. In it, identify when you intend to deploy the assessment and why you are doing it. Include the purpose and goals. Identify why the raters' feedback is important. Identify the name of the assessment. Keep your message short and to the point.

Pre-deployment

Make certain you develop a Welcome or introductory message. Identify the name of your assessment and what you want raters to do. Identify whether and/or how raters can enter and exit whenever they want. Let raters know they can change their responses. Identify the assessment's length and how long it will take them on average to complete it. Provide them with instructions about how they can get started. Do they need an ID and password? Or can they simply click on a link such as "Click Here to Begin" to start? Who can they contact if they have questions or a problem?

Welcome

Develop a Follow-Up Reminder message. Your software should be able to send automated follow-up messages at a pre-set interval, e.g., every twenty-four, forty-eight, seventy-two, or ninety-six hours. You can send these messages to every rater or only to those who have yet to complete and return their responses. There are pros and cons to each option.

Follow-Up Reminder

The safest approach is to send the message to all raters, without identifying delinquent raters. The downside is that everyone will get the message, even those who completed it. This is a bit like receiving an "if the check is in the mail" notice after you have paid the invoice. Some folks will simply delete the follow-up message and go about their business because they have done what was expected of them. Other folks will go supersonic whenever they receive *another* e-mail message because they are soooooo busy. Rather than simply completing the survey (or deleting the follow-up message), they might spend time ragging on the person who sent the message. Well, they can't be all that busy if they can find the time to dump on someone; dizzy, yes, but busy, no!

It is more efficient to send follow-up reminders only to those outstanding raters. However, you then risk having people question your process. *How did they know I did not complete my survey? Isn't this anonymous?* Follow up only with outstanding raters unless there is a climate of absolute mistrust and apprehension about the motives and true intentions of your feedback process. Does your software give you both of these options?

In the end, I recommend that you send your follow-up messages to outstanding raters only because this is the most efficient. Raters have a choice: complete the assessment or decline it. So long as they choose to procrastinate they will receive follow-up messages. As noted, the downside is that some raters will go paranoid and wonder, *"How do they know I didn't complete this?"*

Up-front positioning can ensure greater success for your 360-degree project.

Decline Option

Consider including a decline option when raters open the assessment. They can choose to start it or choose not to complete it at all. When raters select "Decline," they will not receive any follow-up messages and they will no longer be allowed to enter and/or complete the survey. I recommend using some tough love here. Now, you may feel that this is not a viable option. You may believe it is the divine obligation of raters to provide feedback. Okay, but consider this: if that rater is forced to provide the feedback, how relevant will the feedback be? Will the rater provide open and honest feedback or will (s)he just check off a response to get it done? Raters may believe it is their divine right to refuse to participate, for whatever reason.

Up-Front Positioning

What if your organization has not used a 360-degree assessment survey? What if the process of giving formal feedback is too new, too scary, or too different from what you typically do? What if you have not conducted formal performance appraisals with your employees (or do so sporadically)? Up-front positioning can help you establish trust in the process, for the assessment, for you (or the author), for your department (e.g., HR or Personnel), and for your organization.

Schedule a series of meetings with those who will be assessed as well as with those who will be asked to provide participants with feedback. Typically, either an external consultant or someone from HR does this. Do this face-to-face if logistically possible. Conduct thirty- to sixty-minute positioning sessions with as many employees as you can and segregate the sessions. In one session include only the participants; in another session, include only the bosses or team leaders of those participants. In a third session, include the direct reports or team members. If you intend to include external customers, send them a short letter identifying why you want and need their open and honest feedback. You do not need face-to-face meetings. An upper-level manager should sign this letter. Select someone who customers recognize, someone they can relate to and respect. If logistics are an issue, consider Web-conferencing, e-mails, newsletters, and regular old memos. When employees are in different locations, electronic positioning options may be the most cost-effective ways to let folks know about your assessment process.

The focus of each positioning session will vary according to your audience. Consider these suggestions to create your own positioning agenda, given your audience and objectives. Select what you believe is important to communicate during each positioning session.

- What is 360-degree feedback?
- How does the 360-degree process differ from what you are doing now?
- Why are you doing this?
- Why have you decided to do this now?
- What's in it for each rater group?
- What are the benefits for completing the assessment to participants, raters, teams, work units, and the organization as a whole?
- How will participants benefit from the feedback?
- Which participants or departments will be selected first and why?
- Whose feedback do you want (internal, external)?
- Who will select the raters?
- How many raters should be selected (for confidentiality, meaningful results)?

- What do you expect participants to do with their feedback results?
- What is the length and average time to complete this survey?
- When would you like raters to complete their survey (e.g., within forty-eight hours)?
- Will you send follow-up reminders to outstanding raters (or to everyone)? How often will these be sent?
- Will raters be allowed to decline the survey?
- Will raters be allowed to select a "not-applicable" response to any item?
- Who can raters contact with questions, concerns, and problems?
- Who will see the feedback results?
- When will they see their results?
- Will responses be kept confidential and anonymous?
- How can raters be sure?
- How will you protect the anonymity of the raters (especially direct reports and customers)?
- Can raters enter and exit whenever they want? Will their data be saved?

Let all raters understand that their responses should be open and honest, and that this assessment is not an opportunity to get even with anyone. Raters should think about a participant's behavior over time and not be influenced by a one-time event, positive or negative, as they respond to each item. This is an opportunity to help the participant identify his/her strengths and developmental needs. This is not a time to be overly nice or overly vindictive. This is not a time to vent one's anger against the organization in general or against a particular individual. This is an opportunity for the organization to roll up the data and identify any needed training and development programs that would benefit the employee population in general.

Include in your up-front positioning sessions the expectations you have of the immediate managers—the favorite bosses of participants. Some modicum of accountability is in order. The immediate manager is responsible for helping his/her people reach their potential. When a boss's people succeed, so does the boss. Set expectations up front. Should bosses meet with participants to discuss participant feedback results within one week? Should bosses agree to coach and mentor the participant where applicable? Some

managers may need training to become more effective coaches. Do they know how to help their people create action plans? Are they aware of the training programs HR has to offer? Are they willing to help their people reach their potential? No? Why not? When the boss chooses not to do this, or does not have the ability to do this, then human resources needs to step in and assign someone to do that. Identify this option or alternative up front.

Does HR have developmental programs to help participants in the areas they need development? Do participants know this? If not, will participants be able to go outside of your organization for the programs they need? If so, who foots the bill, your department or the participant? It serves little use for participants to receive feedback and then not be given the resources to build on their strengths and resolve any identified weaknesses.

We recently conducted an on-site positioning session with one of our clients in city government. With our client's help, support meetings were scheduled with the participants. The one-hour meeting began with an introduction by the city manager, discussing his experience with one of our 360-degree assessments and why he was expanding the process to the next level, i.e., to these participants. I then highlighted who we are, our experience with performance-based 360-degree feedback, how our process would be administered to them and their respective raters, and the developmental focus of the entire process. I responded to questions and made recommendations about the types of raters to include and how to create sub-groups for their direct reports and peers for more focused feedback. I then met with the raters for these participants. The city manager again introduced me and related his experiences with our feedback process. He then left the meeting. During this forty-five-minute meeting I responded to their questions, which centered primarily on confidentiality and anonymity issues and what participants were expected to do with the results. I emphasized that this was a developmental process and that participants would be expected to share their results, create action plans, and generally identify what they could be doing differently to work more effectively with them. I also emphasized that raters should not think of the worst experiences when they completed the assessment, but rather think in terms of "overall experiences" they had had with the person they were about to assess. The participants were not included in this meeting. We deployed the assessment three days after this meeting. The return rate from all raters was 98.6 percent, which is close to excellent. Only two raters chose not to complete their assessment. Superb commitment! Superb response!

Rater Biases

Raters bias can be

positive and negative.

You can make it difficult (and almost impossible) for raters to gang up against a participant with a well-designed Web-based system. Yet raters can be biased towards the participant all by their lonesome. Rater biases can be both positive and negative. They can skew the results. But bias is a fact of who we are. You can ameliorate some (most?) biases by identifying them to raters during pre-deployment positioning meetings. You could include some mention in your initial instructions, though that would add to those instructions. You can also just ignore the issue of rater bias. I consider rater bias a non-issue. Yet it is our practice to let raters know that a single event can cloud their entire assessment of the participant and result in a biased assessment. Some of the most common biases are called effects: Halo, Horns, and Pygmalion, and the ever popular, cognitive dissonance.

The **Halo effect** can skew responses when a person is positively influenced by a specific event. That is, if a person's impression of the participant is that (s)he is a good listener, the rater may conclude that the participant is good at other modes of communication, such as speaking and writing. If a rater believes that a tall person looks like a leader and tallness is a central trait of leaders in general (or this specific tall participant in particular), then a rater will view other traits associated with this tall person as leadership traits and will respond accordingly, i.e., positively. A single strong point or trait can influence a rater's perception of this person positively, thus the label for this effect.

The **Horns effect** is the opposite of the Halo effect. A person who has an undesirable trait or habit is then viewed as having many other negative traits and habits. A single, strong negative point can influence a rater's overall perception. If a person finds someone's dress or hygiene habits to be sloppy or not acceptable, that person will find other unrelated traits and habits sloppy or undesirable as well. Say you are about to inherit a new boss. You do not know this person. You two have not met. You have been told that (s)he is meticulous and detail oriented. If you think these are positive attributes, what impressions do you think you will form, sight unseen? Think Halo effect. If you view these as negative attributes, what will your impressions be? This is the Horns effect.

The **Pygmalion effect** comes about as a result of the expectations one person has of another person. Think *My Fair Lady* or George Bernard Shaw. People perform in ways that are consistent with others' expectations of them. This works both ways. If a person believes that their direct reports are borderline village idiots and are pushing two-digit IQs and have problems remembering their names without cue cards, that person will almost certainly lower any performance expectations for those direct reports. That person will almost always look over the shoulders of those direct reports and check up on how and what they are doing, and spoon-feed them information that the person thinks they can handle.

A person's expectations, high or low of someone, affect that person's self-confidence and self-image. If you believe the person is a self-starter and delivers high quality work the first time, on time, you will tend to give him/her a free rein in how (s)he completes a task. When you praise someone more frequently than you do others or include them in your problem-solving meetings, you build his/her self-image and confidence with respect to, say, solving problems. While you may not realize the impact your words and actions have on others, folks pick up on your behavior quickly. There is a self-fulfilling prophecy at work here. If you believe that I am not an effective speaker, then whenever I speak before a group you will find faults with my presentation and justify your perceptions, saying something like, "Well, I always knew you had problems thinking on your feet while speaking to a group of your peers." Conversely, if you believe I am an excellent

Raise the bar for all your direct reports. Raise your expectations so they can raise their performance.

speaker, when I make a mistake or are a little slow responding to a question, you will look past it (and perhaps think of blaming the person who asked the question and put me on the spot).

And speaking of raising the bar . . . when I was in high school I played different sports. One was track and field, the low hurdles in particular. One fine day I wanted to take a shot at the high hurdles. My coach wasn't so sure, but gave me the opportunity anyway. Initially, I could clear the hurdles, but mostly they seemed to find their way into my thighs and elsewhere. After falling, I would get up and my coach would remind me that the object was to clear the hurdle, to go over it without hitting it, and that if I kept hitting the hurdles my voice would change, or something like that. (I had a deep voice then as now.) For a while every time I went out to practice I recalled my coach's comments. And every time I smacked a hurdle he would say something like "Congratulations! You screwed up again." He said this in a very high voice, for my amusement I am sure. Within the month I convinced myself that a deeper voice was the better part of valor. I left the high hurdles. I left the low hurdles. I left anything that looked like a hurdle. I suddenly had a strong interest in cross-country running. Sometimes when you believe the negative things folks say about you or allow people to influence you in a negative way, you lose confidence in yourself and believe those negative things. Sometimes when folks say you can't do something and you believe them, you stop trying and lose the opportunity to excel in something. It can happen!

Psychological hurdles can be more difficult to overcome than physical barriers.

We often have **cognitive dissonance** about our actions regarding things. We often buy things that we do not really need, then experience some anxiety or stress or conflict as a result. There is inconsistency between our beliefs and our actions. We buy monster gas guzzlers, feel funny all over a little later, then buy subscriptions to *Going Greenie* magazine and feel better. We talk PC to someone when we would really like to say they are a brick short of a full load. This tends to make you feel uncomfortable. You say the food your host has prepared is really interesting, when you really want to compare its taste and texture to fermented wallpaper paste. We know a person's performance is poor but cannot find the hormones to express it face-to-face or say so on her/his performance appraisal, so we give the person vanilla feedback on his/her appraisal and invite him/her to lunch.

A team member knows another team member is a poor performer and indicates that on the 360-degree assessment, then feels guilty about providing that feedback to the person. So, the team member who provided the feedback acts overly nice to the poor performer, hoping the latter will not identify the former as the one who provided the feedback.

To Bribe or Not to Bribe

Should you consider offering raters an incentive to complete their assessment? Absolutely not! People are going to complete the questions or they won't. Incentives are bribes, plain and simple. If you need to bribe people or offer them some sort of incentive such as a piece of candy, a cutesy trinket, or money, how valuable will their data be anyway? Of course, many people believe it is possible to buy (i.e., bribe) a person with money. Say it isn't so! Well, you can see where this could lead. You offer folks a buck or some trinket now, and pretty soon it escalates. They will expect a little warm fuzzy something just to show up to work. That is when you have created an entitlement program. If they reach upper management they may expect an outrageous compensation package; they may expect a parachute or something. Some may even strive for mediocrity, provide minimal leadership, and demand a ridiculous severance package not based on performance but based on just because.

So, just put your survey out there. Think tough love once again! Draw an adult line in the sand! Make it easy for them to understand what you want them to do. Position the process so they understand the value to those who provide the feedback and those who are being assessed. Allow them to decline to complete the survey if they are that nervous or indifferent or busy or dizzy or whatever. Send out follow-up reminders to all outstanding raters. You may not get a 100 percent response. Yet the data you get may be much more valid than those from a bribe.

Bribery can influence rater bias. Some raters may feel obligated to provide "nice feel-good feedback" because of the incentive they received. Others may see the incentive for what it is: a bribe. They become outraged and indignant and

Should you provide incentives to complete your assessments? No!

in a vengeful sort of way provide "nasty feedback" to demonstrate what they think of such incentives and foolishness. Others, of course, will pocket the bribe and think they just got lucky and will complete the assessment as they would whether they received the incentive or not.

Our research and experience suggest that the quicker raters respond, the greater their comfort level with the 360-degree process and their willingness to provide feedback to another person. The longer it takes them to respond, the less comfy they are with the process and the less likely they will provide open and honest feedback. The longer it takes the participant to self-assess, the greater the tension level with the process and how their feedback will compare with the perceptions of others. The longer it takes favorite bosses to respond, the greater their level of tension with the 360-degree process, especially if the feedback does not match the feedback they provided on a recent performance appraisal. The longer it takes direct reports to respond, the greater their level of mistrust with the process and the less comfy they are providing their boss (i.e., the participant) with open and honest feedback. And the longer it takes participants to share their results with others, say their favorite boss, the less pleased they are with the results and the more likely that their results were more negative than they had anticipated or thought possible.

How to Prevent Apathy and Boredom

- Avoid asking the same question in different ways.
- Include multiple questions on the computer screen to minimize scrolling.
- Do not allow any questions to wrap to a second screen.
- Highlight any unanswered or skipped questions so raters can quickly locate and complete them.
- Allow raters to exit and re-enter the survey.
- Allow raters to review and change any of their responses.
- Make certain you identify the relationship of the rater to the person being evaluated on each screen of your assessment. The stronger the relationship, the higher the response rates (typically).
- Send follow-up reminder messages to all outstanding raters to remind them why their feedback is important to the participant.

Lack of Rater Response

Have you ever wondered why some people complete an assessment and others do not? Or why some people think the whole concept of 360-degree feedback is just so much bother, just one more HR initiative they label "Who Cares?" There could be several legitimate reasons. Lack of trust could be one reason.

If you have used feedback in a way that is perceived as criticism or as a way to reduce your overhead, then your employees will not trust you. If the enlightened boss has created exciting ways to get even with employees for providing open and honest feedback, raters may decide that skittishness is the better part of valor. People simply may not want to participate in the process.

Another reason could be that employees have a lot of these assessments to complete. Some raters may be asked to respond to multiple surveys from different participants within the organization. They may feel overwhelmed or simply bored by having to complete several within a short time frame. They respond to some and delete or ignore the others. As a result, some folks may have inadvertently deleted their e-mail message and the link to the survey *by accident*. How many assessments will any one person have to complete? That depends on who selected which raters for each tracking form. No rater should complete more than two assessments in any given day. If a rater has ten (or more) to complete, suggest they complete one per day over a two-week period. You may need to extend the due date by an extra week or two to accommodate those folks with multiple assessments to complete, folks who travel, and so on.

Another reason for low rater response could be a lack of follow-up in the past. If you asked customers for feedback and then failed to provide them with a summary of the results or some other follow-up action, they may not see the need to take the time to complete another assessment.

You can take several positive steps to increase internal and external rater response. Think through your project from beginning to end. Ask yourself (and be able to respond to) these basic questions:

- You do have the support and active involvement of top management, right? And you know this how?
- The purpose of the 360-degree feedback process is developmental, right?
- You are waiting at least one year before considering the 360 data for your performance management-compensation process, right?
- You addressed concerns about confidentiality of data, right?
- You conducted positioning sessions with employees, right?
- You are going to allow participants to see their data first, right?
- You are not using the feedback results to punish, criticize, ridicule, transfer, or terminate the employee, right?

Office politics aside, our research indicates that participants value feedback from their direct reports first, their bosses second, and their peers third. Participants believe the most accurate feedback comes from those who observe them the most often, i.e., their direct reports, followed by their bosses, and then peers. Likewise, they believe their direct reports, followed by the bosses and peers, are in the best position to observe their leadership behaviors and practices. Participants who refer to their direct reports or staff as subordinates typically do not value feedback from these sources as much as a from other rater groups.

Administration and Administrators

I am separating the design and development tasks from administrative tasks, though the same person could do all of these. I have included an administrator checklist in the Appendix. The administrator is the person who enters your assessment onto the software. It is now Web-enabled. The administrator keeps your project running smoothly through your Web-based software. The administrator is a non-technical person. The administrator also:

- Uploads the names and e-mail addresses of all participants and raters.
- Deploys the assessment.
- Provides status reports.
- Keeps you informed about how things are going.
- Creates the feedback profiles.
- Forwards those profiles to each participant and/or to authorized personnel.
- Is the person who has direct access to the software and can view the feedback results from any participant if (s)he so desires.

Notes:

Module Focus

Delivering the feedback results to participants in one-on-one and group sessions; identifying the four (plus one) types of feedback participants receive; displaying the individual and group feedback results; the value of pre and post assessments; creating resource guides within your feedback software.

PERSPECTIVES

DESIGNING IT

DEVELOPING IT

DEPLOYING IT

DELIVERING IT

Options for Deliverance

egardless of the format you use to deliver the feedback results, participants must understand:

- Their results.
- The consequences of their behavior.
- The consequences of building on their strengths and resolving their weaknesses.
- The next steps towards building on their strengths and resolving their weaknesses.

Support materials are important for guiding participants through their data. Your materials can include:

The participants' personalized *feedback profile* (the results).
An interpretation guide for interpreting each reporting format.
Self-directed action planning forms.

So how will participants receive their results? Who, if anyone, will also receive those results, and when? Let's say you are about to present information to participants. How will you do that so they are comfortable with the process? Have you thought about how you will deal with the sheer joy and exuberance participants experience when they receive highly positive feedback? What about their feelings bordering on sheer terror when the results are not so highly positive? How you present the results to participants is critical for gaining the most from the feedback process. Some organizations have a structured process. Others take a figure-it-out-for-yourself approach. There are at least five formats to consider.

1. Self-instructional: Participants receive their deliverables, e.g., feedback profiles, interpretation guides, and self-directed action planning forms, electronically by e-mail. Participants can print these or you could print them and distribute them to each participant. Whether participants view their results online or on paper, this format requires that they review and analyze their results, create self-directed action plans, and share their results and plans with others. Participants do not have to attend a workshop. There is less out-of-production time and no travel expenses. Participants often like this method because they can procrastinate dealing with the results as long as they want. They may not have to do anything with the data anyway (if there is no accountability to do so). And they can always say they did not receive the electronic file or they misplaced their hard copies as they wish. These excuses increase when the data is not what participants expected. These excuses increase when participants realize they are only legends in their own mind. These excuses increase when they realize they may be a fan club of one!

At one time or another, we are all legends in our own mind.

2. Structured One-on-One Meetings: Participants receive their profiles and supporting materials when they meet with whoever is qualified to guide the participant through the data. This facilitator can be an internal or external consultant, coach, mentor, or someone from personnel. You can combine formats 1 and 2 if you prefer. Some clients want the participant to review her/his data and become generally familiar with it on their own time, e.g. format 1. Then within the week, participants meet one-on-one with the qualified facilitator. The facilitator guides the participant through the data, helping participants create one to three action plans. Participants often like this because they can share some thoughts without being compromised. Participants like this because they have a captive listener. But organizations do not always like this because it is labor intensive, time consuming, and more expensive. Each facilitator can only meet with one participant at a time. These sessions can be as short as thirty minutes or as long as three hours, depending on budget, title of the participant, level of acceptance or denial of the data, and propensity to go off on war-story tangents, and so on.

3. Structured Workshop: Participants receive their profiles and materials during a half- or full-day feedback interpretation session. A qualified facilitator guides participants through the different reporting formats and helps them create at least one action plan each. The workshop includes between ten to twenty-four participants. The facilitator explains the data for each reporting format once, using generic examples. This format allows the facilitator to share the group roll-up, that is, the aggregated strengths and weaknesses of the group as a whole. A structured workshop is usually more cost effective. One facilitator can easily work with many participants during the same time period. It allows for group dynamics, especially when it comes to sharing the feedback and creating action plans. A wide variety of individual, group, and roundtable exercises can be included, allowing participants to see beyond their data and think in terms of next steps. They can identify what they intend to do differently as a result of their feedback. They can also commiserate and celebrate with one another.

4. Combination: Workshop and One-on-One Coaching:
Combining a structured workshop, e.g. format 3, followed immediately by one-on-one coaching sessions helps participants understand their strengths and developmental needs. You can conduct your workshop in the morning and begin your scheduled one-on-one coaching sessions in the afternoon right after feeding time. It allows for group interaction and private discussion time. Participants identify the key behaviors they intend to include in their action plans. The coaching sessions are about thirty to forty-five minutes (at least initially). This structured combination allows participants to get as much out of the process as possible in a relatively short period of time. There is interaction with one's peers and private interaction with the facilitator or coach. These sessions are not opportunities for the participant to pull you or the facilitator off track, however. It is not an opportunity to complain about the inequities in life. Facilitators using any of these format options need to keep the focus on the participants' feedback and what they intend to do differently as a result of that feedback.

5. Combination: Self-Instruction Format 1, Workshop and One-on-One Coaching Format 4: As you see, you can combine different formats to suit your objectives and to take into account your budget and logistical constraints. Participants can review and analyze their data in a self-instructional format three to four days prior to your scheduled workshop. They can identify areas of clear strengths and weaknesses, and identify those areas of confusion for further clarification. During the workshop the facilitator can summarize each reporting format and focus on more of the application of the results and next steps for applying what they have learned. Prior to the concurrent one-on-one coaching session, participants identify their top three to six areas of strengths and weaknesses. They

identify with whom they intend to share their results and when. During the one-on-one coaching session, discussion can focus more on how each participant will share his/her results and how each intends to modify their behavior to eliminate or minimize weaknesses.

Evaluate the Process

Once you decide on and implement the format that is best for your organization, include an evaluation at the end of the project so you can identify what went well and what did not go as well as you had hoped. Consider these questions as a starting point:

Mirror, mirror on the wall, how am I doing, overall? If I need to change, can I stall? If I stall, will my career hit the wall?

- What did people like and dislike about the process?
- Were the directions clear?
- Was the survey easy to complete?
- What did participants learn about themselves?
- What do participants intend to do as a result of their data?
- What would participants do differently with respect to rater selection the next time?
- What would you do differently the next time you deploy this or any other survey?
- What went well?
- How can you build on these strengths?
- What disasters did you experience?
- What did you learn from this first deployment?

Four Types of Feedback (Plus One)

Participants receive different types of feedback. Participants want to know what are their strengths and weaknesses. This is the basic feedback. How you present that information is a function of your software. Provide participants with at least four primary types of feedback: strengths, hidden strengths, developmental needs, and discrepancies. A fifth type of feedback focuses on areas for clarification. Each type allows participants to understand the consequences of their behavior. Participants can apply what they learn from their feedback results in a variety of ways.

CCi SURVEYS INTERNATIONAL: DIRECTIONAL FEEDBACK RESULTS	
STRENGTHS The participant and another rater group(s) agree that this behavior is a strength to build upon.	**DEVELOPMENTAL NEEDS** The participant and another rater group(s) agree that a specific behavior is an area for improvement and development.
HIDDEN STRENGTHS The participant believes (s)he needs to improve but another rater group(s) sees this behavior as a strength to build upon.	**DISCREPANCIES** The participant believes this behavior is a solid strength and that no improvement is needed, yet another rater group(s) sees this as an area for improvement and development.

Strengths: These are behaviors and practices that the participant and at least one other rater group identified as highly effective. The participant is meeting the expectations of this particular rater group. The participant sees this as a personal strength. *These are effective behaviors that I and this rater group agree upon.* Take advantage of these strengths and build upon them to remain effective. No change in behavior is recommended. The participant deserves a little warm fuzzy or something.

Hidden Strengths: These are behaviors and practices that the participant believes (s)he needs to improve upon, but at least one other rater group sees as highly effective. *These are behaviors I do not see as being effective, but this rater group sees these as effective.* These are positive blind spots to build upon. No change in behavior is recommended. The participant may have higher expectations than others. The participant deserves another little warm fuzzy or something.

Developmental Needs: These are behaviors about which there is alignment between the participant and another rater group(s). Both the participant and another rater group(s) identified this behavior as a weakness and an area for development. *These are behaviors that I and others believe I should develop to become more effective.* These are areas for action planning. A change in behavior is recommended and the participant realizes (s)he needs to do things differently, e.g., do more or do less of that behavior. (S)he will know where (s)he needs to improve and is willing to do what it takes. The participant should get another warm fuzzy or something.

So what you are telling me is that not doing anything to resolve your weaknesses has not helped you work more effectively with others?

Discrepancies: These include behaviors and practices that the participant believes (s)he does very effectively, but another rater group(s) does not see the behavior as effective. *These are behaviors that I believe I do well but this rater group sees these same behaviors as weaknesses and believes I should develop to become more effective.* These are negative blind spots. These are toughies for many participants to accept. This is nasty business, this feedback stuff. *I think I am terrific, just ask me. I know I am effective. I've heard myself say that a lot of times to folks.* Others have a different opinion. No fuzzies or warm somethings this time.

Clarifications: This is a fifth type of feedback. This type applies only to those rater groups with two or more raters, such as direct reports, peers, team members, internal or external customers. This feedback identifies *intra-rater group inconsistencies.* Within a rater group there may be disagreement regarding the participant's effectiveness for a specific behavior. Some raters within that group, say the participant's direct report group, may want him/her to *do more* of that behavior. Other raters within that group may want him/her to *do less* of that same behavior. There could also be some raters who see this behavior as one of the participant's strengths. They recommend (s)he *build on this* behavior. There are different expectations within this group(s). There is *intra-rater group inconsistency.* These expectations can be confusing with respect to whether the participant needs to build on this behavior or do more or do less of it.

This type of feedback can present a problem to participants. Many people like their world cut and dried: the lights are on or they are not; we made a profit or we did not. Clarifications upset that tidy world. Highly analytical and logical folks often have problems with this. Clarifications mean that not all of your direct reports, for example, have the same expectations, they are different people with different needs. Many training programs talk about the *one best way to manage others,* but there is no one best way to manage others, much less anything else. Some managers see their direct reports or peers as a homogeneous group, as being the same. They are not. This bit of reality tends to unnerve some folks; it makes their world less black and white and predictable. It turns to gray. As a result, they spend more time analyzing this type of feedback (and guessing who said what) than focusing on the much clearer developmental feedback and the even more difficult feedback to accept — discrepancies.

Data highlighted for clarification identifies how many raters in that group (not by name) believe the participant could do more of this behavior and how many people believe (s)he could do less of this behavior, for example. There is no clear direction for change. The recommended action plan at this point in time is to follow up with that rater group to *clarify* what the participant could be doing differently to work more effectively with them. The results of that meeting can help the participant create a more relevant action plan. (S)he may decide to follow up with that rater group on that behavior only if the behavior or practice is critical to the participant's overall effectiveness and/or whether (s)he believes it is a high priority to follow up with that rater group.

Presentation Options

A *report* is one way to present data to someone. A report can include numbers, text, or combinations of both. A report typically can stand alone. A *profile* includes more than one report and provides participants with multiple ways (reports) for analyzing their feedback results. Each report cuts the data differently and/or presents the same data differently. Generally, you can present data in at least three ways: raw data, directional data, or prescriptive data.

Raw Data: Numerical data is displayed in columns or on spreadsheets. Charts and graphics may be used. Faced with raw data, the participants will have to sort through the numbers and come to their own conclusions. The software organizes and displays the data but does not interpret the results.

Developmental Directional Data: Numerical data is displayed graphically. Some vendors use the phrase "descriptive data" or "descriptive feedback" or "developmental data." Data is displayed while identifying what participants may need to do differently to work more effectively with each rater group. They identify items participants need to *do more of, less of,* and what to *build upon* where no change in behavior

There is no one best way to do anything.

If you don't know where you need to go, then any way will get you somewhere.

is recommended for each rater group. Directional data can include both summaries and detailed item analysis reports. Data is analyzed for participants, yet allows the participants to come to their own conclusions based on the rater group and response distributions for each behavior. Participants create self-directed action plans from the recommendations. Directional data has a situational component to it. Participants can modify their behavior for each rater group. They can modify their behavior for different sets of raters, i.e., subgroups, who share the same function and with those who are located in different areas, for example.

Developmental Prescriptive Data: Often called "prescriptive feedback," this type of data includes specific developmental recommendations for each behavior on the assessment. Participants can integrate the recommendations into their action plans. Receiving the recommendations are not contingent upon attending a workshop or chatting with a trainer or coach. The recommendations are fixed for each item and, therefore, are not tailored to any one participant. Some vendors and software programs include all recommendations for all behaviors regardless of whether they were identified as weaknesses or not. Other vendors and software programs provide more flexibility and display recommendations for only those behaviors that the participant needs to develop. You can select a specific number of items and include their appropriate recommendations or select just a specific percentage of items. Recommendations can be updated and revised as needed. Organizations can integrate key learning points from their training programs with each competency and behavior, as relevant.

A variation of this type of data combines directional feedback with specific prescriptive recommendations for *doing more of, doing less of,* and *building on strengths* for each behavior.

The 360-Degree Feedback Profile

Apart from authors of 360-degree feedback articles, books and assessment tools, who does not have some weaknesses? Perfectionists aside (please!), everyone could improve upon something. Receiving feedback can be overwhelming, especially if that feedback is not what the participant is expecting. There are psychological barriers that can prevent participants from understanding their feedback, let alone accepting their results. There are also presentation barriers that can make it confusing for participants to understand what it is they have before them. There are a wide range of reporting formats that can help participants understand their feedback. This is where you come in, when you were designing your feedback process and building or buying your Web-based software!

What's your pleasure? Do you have a preference for numbers or pretty graphics? You can choose to display data in a way that smacks of entertainment, that provides for more serious analysis, or that is a combination (in case you waffle between the two). You've got your pyramids, regular old tube charts, snappy 3-D tube charts, horizontal bar charts, vertical bar charts, horizontal and vertical stacked bars, line charts, line and bar stacked charts, pareto charts, area charts, bubble charts, candlestick charts, pie charts, spider graphs, scatter grams, histograms, text-words only, and of course those snappy columns of numbers that arouse the most socially dormant. There are a wide range of readily available reporting formats, including off-the-shelf software programs. Most Web-based platforms include built-in reporting formats that you could live with. You may have a choice about the types of reports you can use.

Consider presenting the feedback in different reports, from one-page summaries to multi-page detailed item analyses, from text-only to graphic reports. Including multiple reports will help participants understand their data. They see the consequences of their behavior from different perspectives. Different types of reports can span the range of style

We all want feedback, as long as it mirrors our self-perception.

preferences of your target population. Do they like colored graphics? You can put that in there. Do they like data in columns so they can do the math? Well, you can put that in there as well. Do they like text-only reports? Put that in also.

Reporting Formats

You can use one software platform to design, develop, deploy, administer, and deliver the results from any feedback project. You can choose to export or manually enter the data from that software to another program if you are so inclined. Perhaps that program provides more or different reporting formats. Consider software that is a comprehensive and self-contained platform. This will save you time.

How you can display the results is contingent upon your software. Some typical Web-based software programs allow you to display the data by:

- Prioritizing top strengths and developmental needs
- Highlighting discrepancies between self and other rater groups
- Highlighting most to least effective competencies
- Highlighting most to least effective behaviors and practices
- Detailed item analysis by behavior
- Directional feedback: do more, do less
- Items to clarify
- Importance ratings
- Comparisons to norms
- Comparisons to an ideal

Help participants understand how their behavior can effect and affect the behavior of others. Help them understand the consequences of their behavior for both themselves and with others. How you present the data will help. Here are some options to consider as a starting point.

Summary Reports

Summary reports, by definition, highlight some key aspects of the total data provided to participants. They are snapshots. They can prioritize a participant's top strengths and developmental needs. They can compare discrepancies between participants' self-ratings and those of the other rater groups. They can summarize areas of importance. They can summarize a participant's most and least effective competencies-themes and/or behaviors. Typically, summary reports or overall average data points do not include the participant's reported self data. Participants tend to skew their results. They see themselves as being much more highly effective or much less effective than do other rater groups. More to the point of 360-degree feedback is the feedback from others. Yes, self data is necessary and important from a reference point of view. Yet it is the observations and input from others that is the critical point for development.

You may want to include an average response in one or more of your reporting formats. Averages allow you to compare items more easily. Depending on how these averages are computed, a low score, i.e., 0.00, could be a solid strength or a major weakness. You may want to know which logic set your vendor uses. Averages are a convenient way to summarize information. You may want to take the time to determine where those averages come from. You need to interpret the numbers behind the averages. You need to look inside those numbers and understand what they are telling you before you encourage participants to forge ahead with an action plan. Some examples of summary reports are:

Overall Results
Overall Importance Ratings
Strengths by Rater Group
Developmental Needs by Rater Group
Strengths by Frequency of Occurrence
Developmental Needs by Frequency of Occurrence

Overall Results

This is a one-page summary that identifies those behaviors that raters indicated were the top (key, critical, core, etc.) strengths and those that were a participant's top weaknesses or areas for development. Ideally, each behavior will be linked to its corresponding competency.

Applications: Participants use this report as a starting point when creating their action plans. They identify the behaviors for their action plans and discuss the availability of any training and development initiatives with HR by competency area. The items on the left side are the behaviors and those on the right are the corresponding competencies.

Prioritize top strengths,

developmental needs.

7/26 CCI Direct Connect Demo - 09/13/2001 Single Participant: Judy Sample	Overall Results	CCI Surveys International Enter your company name here

There are a total of 12 respondents in groups including: Boss A(1), Boss B(1), Staff A(3), Peer A(3), Peer B(4)

Strengths
These are the top 6 behaviors or practices identified by at least 50% of the respondent groups.

10. Make time to speak with colleagues	3. People Skills
9. Accurately summarizes action points resulting from meetings	3. People Skills
15. Balance needs for efficiency with those for effectiveness at work	4. Task Skills
16. Emphasize the standard of quality of my work	4. Task Skills
18. Discuss work issues and problems	5. Collaboration
19. Share ideas for generating revenue for the business	5. Collaboration

Developmental Needs
These are the top 5 behaviors or practices identified by at least 50% of the respondent groups.

12. Brief on work status	4. Task Skills
8. Listen to others' point of view	3. People Skills
11. Respond to colleagues' personal needs as well as their work needs	3. People Skills
5. Give accurate and timely feedback on employees' performance	2. Guiding Others
13. Organize his or her work appropriately	4. Task Skills

Overall Importance Ratings

This is a one-page summary that identifies those competencies rated most important by each rater group and those competencies rated commonly across all rater groups. This type of report does not identify how effectively the participant performs. Rather, it ranks or orders or identifies those competencies deemed more important than others.

Applications: Participants apply this data when they prioritize the behaviors they choose to develop first. An item identified as a top weakness linked to a competency with a high importance rating can be a high priority for action planning. Conversely, an item identified as a weakness, but with a corresponding theme that has a low importance rating, is not yet a high priority for action planning. The participant does not do this behavior effectively but it comes under the priority label of "Who cares?"

Prioritize priorities.

7/26 CCI Direct Connect Demo - 09/13/2001 Single Participant: Judy Sample	Overall Importance Ratings	CCI Surveys International Enter your company name here

By Rater Group	**Self (N=1)** 1. Personal Initiative 3. People Skills	**Boss A (N=1)** 1. Personal Initiative 2. Guiding Others
	Boss B (N=1) 5. Collaboration 1. Personal Initiative	**Staff A (N=3)** 1. Personal Initiative 2. Guiding Others
	Peer A (N=3) 1. Personal Initiative 2. Guiding Others	**Peer B (N=4)** 1. Personal Initiative 2. Guiding Others
By Frequency of Occurrence	Personal Initiative (5) Collaboration (1)	Guiding Others (4)

Strengths by Rater Group and Developmental Needs by Rater Group

These are two separate one- to three-page reports. The former identifies strengths by item-behavior linked to its corresponding competency. The "Developmental Needs by Rater Group" report identifies behaviors that could be included into self-directed action plans. Together, these reports correlate the behavior the participant performs to expectations (strengths) and those that need development (developmental needs), according to each rater group.

Highlight discrepancies

between all rater groups.

Applications: Participants see exactly how many behaviors are strengths to build upon according to each rater group and how many behaviors are weaknesses. The behaviors are linked to their corresponding competency by their numeric sequence in the assessment. Participants can establish patterns among rater groups by identifying how often question number ten, for example, appears as a strength (or developmental area) among the rater groups. Data for each rater group is not co-mingled. Participants can easily create action plans for each rater group if necessary. Depending on the data, these two reports would help participants create specific action plans for working with favorite bosses, or other rater groups.

Strengths by Rater Group

Self (N = 1)
1) Personal Initiative 1,4
2) Guiding Others 7
3) People Skills 10,11
4) Task Skills 12,14,15,16
5) Collaboration 18,19,20

Boss A (N = 1)
1) Personal Initiative 3
3) People Skills 9,10
4) Task Skills 14,15,16
5) Collaboration 18,19,20

Boss B (N = 1)
1) Personal Initiative 2
2) Guiding Others 7
3) People Skills 10
4) Task Skills 14,15,16
5) Collaboration 18,19,20

Staff A (N = 3)
3) People Skills 10,9
4) Task Skills 16,17,15
5) Collaboration 18,19,20
1) Personal Initiative 1
2) Guiding Others 6

Peer A (N = 3)
3) People Skills 9,10
1) Personal Initiative 1,3

Peer B (N = 4)
3) People Skills 10,9
4) Task Skills 16,17,15
5) Collaboration 18,19,20
1) Personal Initiative 1
2) Guiding Others 6

Developmental Needs by Rater Group

Self (N = 1)
2) Guiding Others 6,5
3) People Skills 8,9
1) Personal Initiative 2,3

Boss A (N = 1)
4) Task Skills 12
2) Guiding Others 5
3) People Skills 8,11

Boss B (N = 1)
1) Personal Initiative 3
4) Task Skills 12

Staff A (N = 3)
4) Task Skills 14,12,13
3) People Skills 8,11
2) Guiding Others 5

Peer A (N = 3)
4) Task Skills 12,13,16,17,14
1) Personal Initiative 4
2) Guiding Others 7,5
3) People Skills 11,8
5) Collaboration 18,19,20

Peer B (N = 4)
3) People Skills 8,11
2) Guiding Others 5
4) Task Skills 13,12
1) Personal Initiative 2

Create individualized training needs analyses to identify effective and ineffective behaviors.

Strengths by Frequency of Occurrence and Developmental Needs by Frequency of Occurrence

These are two separate one- to three-page reports. Both reports aggregate the data from all rater groups, except from the participant. Each provides a personalized training and development needs analysis for the participant. "Strengths by Frequency" displays the strengths across all rater groups according to how frequently a specific behavior was identified as a behavior to build upon. The second report, "Developmental Needs by Frequency," displays weaknesses across all rater groups according to how frequently a specific behavior was identified as a behavior to develop.

Applications: Participants use this information to create a single action plan for a specific behavior that applies across all (or most) rater groups. Participants develop action plans for both strengths and weaknesses.

7/26 CCI Direct Connect Demo - 09/13/2001 Single Participant: Judy Sample	**Strengths by Frequency of Occurrence**	CCi Surveys International Enter your company name here

Personal Initiative		
Personal Initiative (5 of 5)	1.	Stress customers in conversations
	3.	Take the initiative to change things that are not effective

People Skills		
People Skills (5 of 5)	10.	Make time to speak with colleagues
	9.	Accurately summarizes action points from meetings

Task Skills		
Task Skills (4 of 5)	15.	Balance needs for efficiency with those for effectiveness at work
	16.	Emphasize the standard of quality of my work
	14.	Make appropriate decisions affecting customers

7/26 CCI Direct Connect Demo - 09/13/2001 Single Participant: Judy Sample	**Developmental Needs by Frequency of Occurrence**	CCi Surveys International Enter your company name here

Task Skills		
Task Skills (5 of 5)	12.	Brief on work status
	13.	Organize his or her work appropriately
	14.	Make appropriate decisions affecting customers

Guiding Others		
Guiding Others (4 of 5)	5.	Give accurate and timely feedback on employees' performance

People Skills		
People Skills (4 of 5)	8.	Listen to others' point of view
	11.	Respond to colleagues' personal needs as well as their work needs

Detailed Reports

Overviews and summary reports can be nice and tidy. Some folks like details. Some folks like to dig into their data and look for subtleties and even come up with their own conclusions. Detailed reports include data for each item on your assessment from each rater group. They can also include detailed importance ratings, and provide directional feedback: do more, do less. Some examples of detailed reports include:

Analysis by Importance Ratings
Analysis by Behavior-Question

Analysis by Importance Ratings

This is a detailed, multi-colored, graphic version of the Overall Importance summary report. This format allows participants to identify the importance ratings for each rater group, compare those ratings among all rater groups (including self ratings), and identify the individual ratings for each rater in each rater group (by response, not name). Participants can identify how many raters (or what percentage of raters) identified a competency as, for example, "Extremely Important" compared to "Not as Important." The graphic illustrates a single-response scale format.

Applications: Participants analyze all importance ratings and identify those competencies that are most important. This report allows participants to see inside their data by providing more details. This report does not refer to performance, only importance. A higher overall average rating (AR) identifies the higher importance of that competency. The competencies identified with the most Xs under the priorities columns have higher importance and should be considered for action planning.

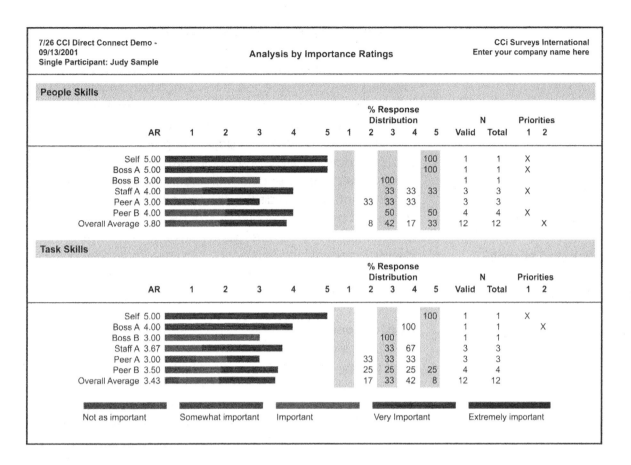

| | 7/26 CCI Direct Connect Demo - 09/13/2001 Single Participant: Judy Sample | | | | | | | Analysis by Importance Ratings | | | | | | | CCi Surveys International Enter your company name here |

People Skills

| | | | | | | | % Response Distribution | | | | | N | | Priorities | |
	AR	1	2	3	4	5	1	2	3	4	5	Valid	Total	1	2
Self	5.00										100	1	1	X	
Boss A	5.00										100	1	1	X	
Boss B	3.00								100			1	1		
Staff A	4.00								33	33	33	3	3	X	
Peer A	3.00							33	33	33		3	3		
Peer B	4.00								50		50	4	4	X	
Overall Average	3.80							8	42	17	33	12	12		X

Task Skills

| | | | | | | | % Response Distribution | | | | | N | | Priorities | |
	AR	1	2	3	4	5	1	2	3	4	5	Valid	Total	1	2
Self	5.00										100	1	1	X	
Boss A	4.00									100		1	1		X
Boss B	3.00								100			1	1		
Staff A	3.67								33	67		3	3		
Peer A	3.00							33	33	33		3	3		
Peer B	3.50							25	25	25	25	4	4		
Overall Average	3.43							17	33	42	8	12	12		

| Not as important | Somewhat important | Important | Very Important | Extremely important |

Provide detailed item-analysis linked to each competency and each rater group.

Create sub-groups, e.g., boss A, boss B, staff A, staff B, customer A, customer B, to provide participants with more specific and more relevant feedback.

Analysis by Behavior-Question

This is one of our signature comprehensive reports. It is a detailed item-analysis report. It links each behavior to its corresponding competency. This multi-page, multi-colored graphic report displays the data for each rater group and identifies any inter-rater gaps. The graphics illustrate our trademark dual-response scale format, comparing observable current behavior with expected behavior. The n-distribution columns display the responses for each rater group, not by name but number (or percent) of respondents, and identify any intra-rater gaps. Participants receive directional feedback and action plan recommendations to *do more of, less of, what to clarify,* and *what to continue doing* and with whom.

Applications: Participants can easily see inside their data. They can analyze each item and the responses of each rater group. Participants can identify data patterns, such as clustering, skewed responses, and bipolar responses. Most participants view their summary data first, then use the detailed item analysis report to come to their own conclusions and/or to confirm what the summary reports indicate. Participants can determine which behaviors to develop with respect to certain rater groups, depending on the data patterns. That is, if the response distributions show that one response in, say, the direct report group, indicates a strong desire for change, but the other responses (raters) do not, participants may not need to create an action plan based on that one response. A single response can skew data, especially when the valid n is less than four raters. Summary reports can point to trends and general conclusions. Detailed item analysis reports identify specific patterns within the data set and identify the extent to which the feedback warrants action planning or a discussion to clarify the data before any action planning takes place.

7/26 CCI Direct Connect Demo - 09/13/2001 Single Participant: Judy Sample	Analysis by Behavior - Question	CCi Surveys International Enter your company name here

Personal Initiative
1) To what extent does this person... Stress customers in conversations

Rater Group	N	AGS	Avg. Gap Size 1	2	3	4	5	N Distribution 0	1	2	3	4	Do Less	Action Plan
Self	1	0.00					◆	1						****
Boss A	1	1.00				C■■■E			1					**
Boss B	1	1.00			C■■■E				1					**
Staff A	3	0.33			C■E			2	1					****
Peer A	3	0.33			C■E			2	1					****
Peer B	4	0.25				C▶E		3	1					****
Overall Average	12	0.42			C■▶E			7	5					****

Personal Initiative
2) To what extent does this person... Learn new tasks

Rater Group	N	AGS	Avg. Gap Size 1	2	3	4	5	N Distribution 0	1	2	3	4	Do Less	Action Plan
Self	1	2.00			C■■■■■E					1				INCREASE
Boss A	1	2.00		E◀■■■C						1			1	DECREASE
Boss B	1	0.00				◆		1						****
Staff A	3	0.67			C■■E			1	2					**
Peer A	3	0.67				C■■▶E		2		1				**
Peer B	4	1.00			C■■■E			1	2	1				INCREASE
Overall Average	12	0.50			C◀■▶E			5	4	3			1	CLARIFY

Current Performance...how often does this occur? = C   1 - Almost Never, 2 - Rarely, 3 - Sometimes, 4 - Usually, 5 - Almost Always
Your Expectations...how often should this occur? = E   1 - Almost Never, 2 - Rarely, 3 - Sometimes, 4 - Usually, 5 - Almost Always

Display Boss Data

Almost every instrument allows you to compare one rater group with another. You can compare the participant with an amorphic group labeled "Others." Displaying data by the "Self" and "Others" categories alone may be fine for self-awareness only, but doing so does not inspire change or act as a catalyst for performance improvement. It may be fine if people within your organization are nervous that the boss's data, for example, will be identified as a separate line item. But this way of presenting data is *feedback-light*. Merging boss data with that of the general category "Others" is too simple and wimpy. The most effective ways to display the data is by "Self" and each of the other rater groups on the survey (e.g., "Self," "Boss," "Staff," "Peers," "Customers," "Team Members," "Co-Workers," "Support," etc.).

Merging "boss" data with other rater groups is feedback-light.

Display Response Distributions

As I mentioned earlier, response distributions help you identify the number of raters whose responses emphasize strengths to build upon or areas to develop. You can identify bipolar data. You can identify skewed responses. You can identify patterns, trends, and the number of raters who responded at the mid-scale point on an odd-response scale, i.e., those who displayed central tendency. Identifying the response distributions for each rater on each item is valuable. Distributions identify whether a rater has skewed his/her response in relation to other raters in that same rater group. Do the majority of raters in the direct report group see the participant as effective? If so, call the participant effective. If the pattern of responses identifies the participant as ineffective (rationalization aside), the participant is ineffective according to that rater group.

Supplemental Reports

There are other reports you may choose to include.
Some of these other options are:

Open-Ended Questions (or Free-Text)
Pre-Post Assessments
Group Reports: Analysis by Behavior
Group Reports: Summary by Theme-Competency
Feed-Forward Resource Guides
   Prescriptive Feedback
   Directional Prescriptive Examples
   Prescriptive Examples

Open-Ended Questions (or Free-Text)

This kind of report includes qualitative comments made by raters. Data is organized according to each open-ended question in the assessment. Individual raters are not identified and rater groups are not identified. Organizing the comments by question rather than raters or their respective group helps ensure anonymity and confidentiality. It also increases the level of trust raters have when they are asked to "Feel free to make any other comments to this participant." Comments are not edited or otherwise manipulated.

Applications: Participants often discover the why behind some of their quantitative data. They often come to the "Aha!" part of their behavior. Qualitative comments can reinforce the quantitative data. As a result, the participant can consider how to address some of these comments in his/her action plan.

Here are two examples to consider. The first example includes qualitative feedback for each item on the assessment. The second example includes the open-ended comments as a separate section in the assessment.

7/26 CCI Direct Connect Demo - 09/13/2001 **Single Participant: Judy Sample**	**Open-Ended Questions**	**CCi Surveys International** Enter your company name here

1) Listen to others' point of view

- I think this person should listen to different points of view, especially mine, because I always have great ideas.
- This person is a wonderful listener now, except of course, when he tunes you out because he doesn't like your ideas.
- Additional comments from additional raters here.
- All open ended comments are randomized to ensure confidentiality.
-
- This is an example of open-ended comments for a specific item on your survey.
- You can use open-ended comments for each item on your survey, each theme on your survey, or create generic open-ended comments, such as What could this person START doing to become more effective; What could this person STOP doing to become more effective; What could this person CONTINUE DOING to become more effective; etc.

2) Accurately summarizes action points resulting from meetings

- I think this person accurately summarizes the action points from meetings whether we want that summary or not. Sometimes the summaries are longer than the meetings.
- This person does such a lovely job summarizing all the trivia from the meetings that often we forget who is responsible for what.
- Additional comments from additional raters here.
- All open ended comments are randomized to ensure confidentiality.
-
- This is an example of open-ended comments for a specific item on your survey.
- You can use open-ended comments for each item on your survey, each theme on your survey, or create generic open-ended comments, such as What could this person START doing to become more effective; What could this person STOP doing to become more effective; What could this person CONTINUE DOING to become more effective; etc.

Leadership Assessment Survey (oeq) - 07/21/2003 **Single Participant: Judy Sample**	**Open-Ended Questions**	**CCi Surveys International** Enter your company name here **Sample Profile**

97) What could this person START DOING to become more effective?

- Be more open to change.
- Openess to change, embrace new ideas.
- Push/implement/sell the ideas that she knows are right even when there is resistance.
- Construct e-mails with concise instructions on tasks, including how the information will be used and for what purpose. This includes e-mails sent on her behalf by her administrative assistant.

  Send e-mails requiring follow-up only to the employees to which it applies.
- More coaching and communicating constructively. Also, loosen the belt and have some fun. It's catchy!
- Nothing really stands out; if pressed, I can only offer that she might hold more frequent feedback sessions on our performance.
- Better represent the Districts to Corp. on issues that are effecting our customers. I'm not sure that Corp. truly understands what is going on in the Districts and how their actions are affecting our day to day relationships with customers. I'm not sure if Judy is carrying our flag or not. If she is, she should better communicate that to us. She also should be more involved in the future direction of the company and how we plan to convert and service our customers in the future. Again, she may be doing this, but we in the field are not aware of her lobbying.
- Better, more consistent feedback. Also, think outside of what we have done in the past.
- It would help me if Judy could provide our group with insight as to some of the direction of the upcoming decisions. Maybe she is being asked not to tell but as a manager I find it difficult to motivate my employees when I cannot help them with the directtion of their own positions. I would like some help with skills I should be working on so I can be more valuable to the business as we have change in the future.
- Be more visible to other areas of the business like product marketing and development (in a positive and cooperative way). Let her creative side shine and be more of a leader - be more outspoken and innovative.

98) What could this person STOP DOING to become more effective?

- Nothing at this point.
- Managing to the group vs managing to the individual. Stop looking at the business from the view of a district, it is much larger than a single district.
- Not get stuck in the "image" of the service org of metrics and reaction
- Sending out e-mails late at night when she is tired and burned out.
- I realize that many of the requests for reports/data/spreadsheets come from HQ and not Judy, but perhaps folks at HQ could do the data mining out of the same data bases we look at, rather than having the field do the digging.
- Advocate for her direct reports to streamline requests, spreadsheets and emails. We have a central repository of info and we should use it more along with the analysts and admins we pay for. Let us spend more time with customers and less time being asked for data.
- Less time on "fires" and more time on fixing process and providing tools. More face time with employees to impart her values.

Pre-Post Assessments

This is another of our signature reports. This detailed, item analysis and multi-colored graphic report compares one assessment (pre) to additional assessments (post) over time all on the same page. It compares each item and identifies the extent to which the participant improved (or did not) since the last assessment. Up to four pre- and post-assessments can be displayed at a time.

Measure progress and results.

Applications: A comparison of baseline data (pre) with current data (post) helps participants measure their progress towards their developmental goals. It can identify the extent to which they have applied what they learned as a result of any training, coaching, and mentoring, and how effectively their application was to any given rater group. Reassessments also identify those behaviors that continue to be viewed as weaknesses and those that continue to be strengths. This type of report is valuable for identifying and confirming high potentials over time, career development, and for succession planning.

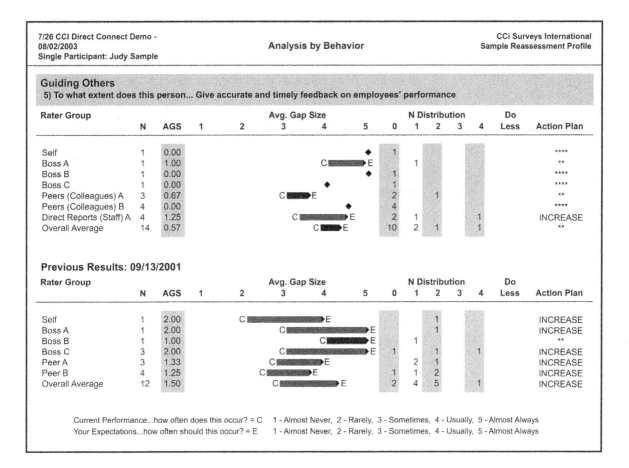

				Avg. Gap Size					N Distribution					Do	

7/26 CCI Direct Connect Demo -
08/02/2003
Single Participant: Judy Sample

Analysis by Behavior

CCi Surveys International
Sample Reassessment Profile

Guiding Others
5) To what extent does this person... Give accurate and timely feedback on employees' performance

Rater Group	N	AGS	1	2	3	4	5	0	1	2	3	4	Do Less	Action Plan
Self	1	0.00					◆	1						****
Boss A	1	1.00				C■■■►E			1					**
Boss B	1	0.00					◆	1						****
Boss C	1	0.00				◆		1						****
Peers (Colleagues) A	3	0.67			C■■►E			2		1				**
Peers (Colleagues) B	4	0.00				◆		4						****
Direct Reports (Staff) A	4	1.25			C■■■►E			2	1			1		INCREASE
Overall Average	14	0.57			C■■►E			10	2	1		1		**

Previous Results: 09/13/2001

Rater Group	N	AGS	1	2	3	4	5	0	1	2	3	4	Do Less	Action Plan
Self	1	2.00		C■■■■■►E						1				INCREASE
Boss A	1	2.00			C■■■■■►E					1				INCREASE
Boss B	1	1.00				C■■■►E			1					**
Boss C	3	2.00			C■■■■■►E			1		1	1			INCREASE
Peer A	3	1.33			C■■■►E				2	1				INCREASE
Peer B	4	1.25		C■■■►E				1	1	2				INCREASE
Overall Average	12	1.50			C■■■■►E			2	4	5	1			INCREASE

Current Performance...how often does this occur? = C 1 - Almost Never, 2 - Rarely, 3 - Sometimes, 4 - Usually, 5 - Almost Always
Your Expectations...how often should this occur? = E 1 - Almost Never, 2 - Rarely, 3 - Sometimes, 4 - Usually, 5 - Almost Always

Group Reports: Analysis by Behavior

Group composites or group profiles or group roll-ups aggregate the data from multiple participants. The data is displayed by rater groups and numbers of raters in each group. Composite data does not identify any single participant by name, but groups of participants. You can create these group composites automatically from your software or create them manually.

Group reports are your training needs analysis for the organization or a specific target population.

Applications: The Analysis by Behavior (and other reports) identify individual strengths and developmental needs of a specific participant. The following examples of the Analysis by Behavior report and the Summary by Theme-Competency report include the feedback from multiple participants. Think of these groups reports and group profiles as your training needs analyses for any demographic you want. Group reports can identify collective strengths to build upon and areas to develop for a specific target population.

Use this information to identify the effectiveness of your training programs or to identify the content areas you may need to add (or delete) from your training programs. Use the group results to identify coaching and mentoring issues. Group profiles, which include multiple reports, can help identify what you may need to do differently during your recruiting and interviewing process. For example, are you selecting people who display the same "weak behaviors" identified in the group data? You can present the data composite in any of the formats described earlier. This report is similar to the Analysis by Behavior for an individual participant. The only difference is that you are looking at the results from multiple participants and their respective raters.

This group report displays the data by each behavior or practice linked to its theme-competency.

Generally, you would share this type of information with key executives and department heads. I highly recommend that you create and share composite results with the participants in your feedback workshop. What's to hide? If there are eighteen participants, roll up their results and present it all as the collective strengths and developmental needs for everyone in that room. The better time to do this is *after* you have explained each reporting format and participants have

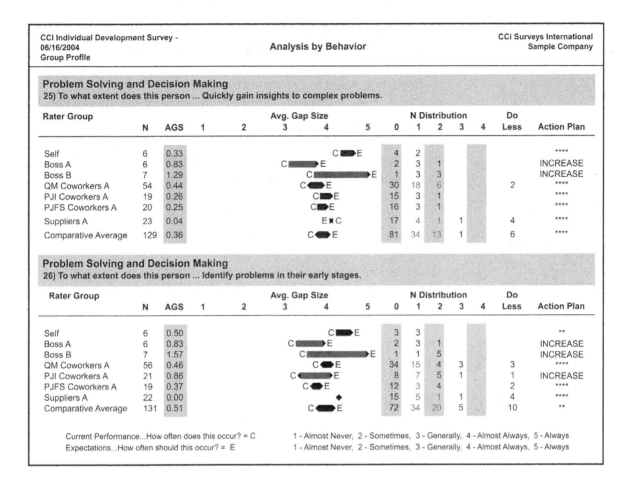

| CCI Individual Development Survey - 06/16/2004 Group Profile | | Analysis by Behavior | | | | | | | | CCi Surveys International Sample Company | |

Problem Solving and Decision Making
25) To what extent does this person ... Quickly gain insights to complex problems.

Rater Group	N	AGS	Avg. Gap Size					N Distribution					Do Less	Action Plan
			1	2	3	4	5	0	1	2	3	4		
Self	6	0.33				C ■■■ E		4	2					****
Boss A	6	0.83		C ■■■■► E				2	3	1				INCREASE
Boss B	7	1.29			C ■■■■■■■■► E			1	3	3				INCREASE
QM Coworkers A	54	0.44			C ◄■■► E			30	18	6			2	****
PJI Coworkers A	19	0.26			C ■► E			15	3	1				****
PJFS Coworkers A	20	0.25			C ■► E			16	3	1				****
Suppliers A	23	0.04			E ◄ C			17	4	1	1		4	****
Comparative Average	129	0.36			C ◄■► E			81	34	13	1		6	****

Problem Solving and Decision Making
26) To what extent does this person ... Identify problems in their early stages.

Rater Group	N	AGS	Avg. Gap Size					N Distribution					Do Less	Action Plan
			1	2	3	4	5	0	1	2	3	4		
Self	6	0.50				C ■■► E		3	3					**
Boss A	6	0.83		C ■■■■► E				2	3	1				INCREASE
Boss B	7	1.57			C ■■■■■■■■► E			1	1	5				INCREASE
QM Coworkers A	56	0.46			C ◄■► E			34	15	4	3		3	****
PJI Coworkers A	21	0.86		C ◄■■■► E				8	7	5	1		1	INCREASE
PJFS Coworkers A	19	0.37			C ◄■► E			12	3	4			2	****
Suppliers A	22	0.00			◆			15	5	1	1		4	****
Comparative Average	131	0.51			C ◄■■► E			72	34	20	5		10	**

Current Performance...How often does this occur? = C   1 - Almost Never, 2 - Sometimes, 3 - Generally, 4 - Almost Always, 5 - Always
Expectations...How often should this occur? = E   1 - Almost Never, 2 - Sometimes, 3 - Generally, 4 - Almost Always, 5 - Always

had time to analyze and process their results, and *before* they are about to launch into developing their action plans.

Share the summary data. Share the top three to six behaviors that the group composite identified as strengths and weaknesses for this group of eighteen. It is not necessary to go through every item on your assessment; that is too much detail and will only sidetrack you. Sharing the group data helps participants realize that other folks in the same room share similar strengths and weaknesses. It helps them buy into their results and be more willing to implement action plans.

Group Reports:
Summary by Theme-Competency

You may need to create your assessment in multiple languages. It would be most beneficial to participants when you can not only collect their feedback in their respective languages, but also present the results to all participants in the languages of their choice. But the argument often goes that all of our managers are fluent in English. Fine. Are they more fluent and more comfortable reviewing their results in, say, English, than in their native language? Include a language option to be a bit more responsive to their comfort level.

Here are three examples of group reports that display the data by theme or competency.

| CCI Direct Connect Demo - 09/13/2001 Single Participant: Judy Sample | | | Summary by Competency - Theme | | | | | CCi Surveys International Sample Report | | | | |

Task Skills

Rater Group	N	AGS	1	2	Avg. Gap Size 3	4	5	N Distribution 0	1	2	3	4	Do Less
Self	6	0.50			E◀━━▶C			4	1			1	1
Boss A	6	0.00			◆			3	1		1	1	1
Boss B	6	0.17			E✕C			3	1	1		1	1
Staff A	18	0.89			C━━━▶E			9	5	2	1	1	
Peer A	17	1.47			C━━━━━━▶E			6	6		1	4	
Peer B	23	0.57			C◀━━━▶E			9	10	2	1	1	1
Overall Average	70	0.76			C◀━━━▶E			30	23	5	4	8	3

Guiding Others

Rater Group	N	AGS	1	2	Avg. Gap Size 3	4	5	N Distribution 0	1	2	3	4	Do Less
Self	3	2.00		C━━━━━▶E				1		1		1	
Boss A	3	1.33			C━━━━▶E					2	1		
Boss B	3	0.67			C━━━▶E			1	2				
Staff A	9	0.67			C◀━━▶E			5	2	1		1	1
Peer A	8	1.38			C━━━━━▶E				5	3			
Peer B	11	0.64			C◀━▶E			4	3	4			1
Overall Average	34	0.88			C◀━━▶E			10	14	9		1	2

Current Performance...how often does this occur? = C   1 - Almost Never, 2 - Rarely, 3 - Sometimes, 4 - Usually, 5 - Almost Always
Your Expectations...how often should this occur? = E   1 - Almost Never, 2 - Rarely, 3 - Sometimes, 4 - Usually, 5 - Almost Always

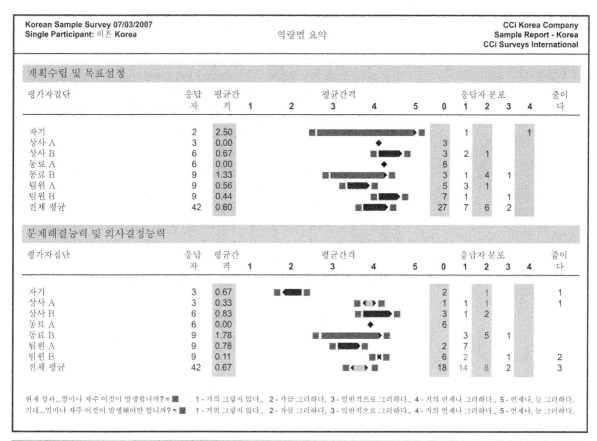

Note: All of your reporting formats should allow the data to be presented in multiple languages (if having multiple languages is applicable to your organization).

Link developmental

recommendations

to each item.

Feed-Forward Resource Guides

Resource guides are good examples of prescriptive feedback. These guides do not typically include numerical data. Rather, they include a wide range of developmental suggestions participants can implement. Link these suggestions to the specific behaviors in your assessment.

When you integrate directional feedback with a resource guide, you create directional prescriptive feedback. Feed-forward and recommendations for development provide participants with what they could be doing differently to work more effectively with others. A resource guide built as an integral part of your software reporting structure can provide participants with developmental tips and recommendations about what they could be doing differently from this point forward. What you include should help participants maximize their performance and effectiveness with others and be relatively easy to implement immediately.

Applications: Participants may not need to attend a training and development program. They can apply the developmental suggestions at any time. Guides can include hyperlinks to any Web-based training program or Web-based resource you can identify. Participants can engage in self-instructional activities when they choose to do so. Guides can integrate key points from your in-house (or external) training programs as well. Resource guides make it easy for participants to take the initiative and engage in developmental activities if they choose to do so.

Prescriptive Feedback

Prescriptive feedback is a one-size-fits-all set of developmental ideas for participants. It can help them improve upon weaknesses. Vendors (or authors of this type of feedback) include a finite number of recommended tips and suggestions for each item in an assessment. All participants who have a specific item listed as a weakness receive the same prescription for doing better. Think of it as a "take-two-aspirins-and-call-me-in-the-morning" prescription. Some vendors include this type of feedback in their ready-to-use assessments for employees to use as starting points for their action plans. By definition, no customized assessment automatically includes these off-the-shelf recommendations. You need to develop them or have them developed for your custom assessment. The recommendations need to be specific given your customized items. Generic recommendations do not quite work with custom items.

Your software may allow you to create your own resource guides, letting you link a set of tips and developmental ideas to each item in your assessment. You can make these ideas more relevant by integrating key points from your training and development programs as they apply to each item. You can include text and drawings and hyperlinks; you can include your online corporate university Web site. Modify your developmental ideas according to any multiple versions of the same basic assessment for different functions or business units.

You do not need to cover the entire waterfront. Include only a sufficient number of ideas and make it easy for participants to apply them. Identify any training and development initiatives you offer to let participants understand that help is available. In addition to providing participants with feedback, you should provide them with the support they may need so they can modify their behavior. Include enough ideas to help them initiate their self-directed action plans without having to wait for your regularly scheduled training program. These developmental ideas can stand alone; they can mirror the language from your training programs that you want to reinforce. Depending on personal initiative, participants may choose to register for your organizational initiatives, such as additional training, coaching, and mentoring. Include a link to do just that in the guide.

As I mentioned, you could print or make available the assessment's entire resource guide to any and all participants, regardless of their developmental needs. Or, depending on the capabilities of your software, you could provide each participant with only those resource guide suggestions that pertain to each of them. The number or percentage of items you include for development can be personalized to each participant. Providing all participants with the entire guide can make sense. Some will appreciate the guide as a future reference. Others, however, will see it as overkill. Yet the option is there for you.

Directional Prescriptive Examples

Resource guides can include as many tips and suggestions as you want. The most relevant guides provide developmental recommendations by item, not by competency or theme. What you include is up to you. If you choose to use a dual-response scale and provide directional feedback, then your resource guide should focus on what the person could *do more* or *less* of for that specific behavior-practice. Include a comment or two about participants' strengths. Reinforce what they are doing well now.

Here are two examples:

. . . .

Example 1
Your assessment Competency-Theme is: Coaching
The item under this competency is: Provide feedback when work does not meet his/her expectations.

Developmental suggestions for this item could include the following:

When raters want you to increase or do more of this behavior: The people who provided you with feedback are asking for more feedback when work does not meet your expectations. Why is that? Some managers may be reluctant to give bad news for fear of upsetting people. Another point to consider is that when you do not let people know immediately that their performance is unacceptable, they will assume that everything is fine and continue to act as they have done before. When you do finally choose to address this situation, it will be difficult to handle because (a) the surprise element will be greater to them and/or (b) the performance may have deteriorated further.

Here are some recommendations as a starting point:

1. Make sure that you have established your own standards of performance and have communicated these to others who are there to provide you with work or a service.
2. Develop a method for measuring output and performance standards. Set clear objectives for your people, so there is little room for multiple interpretations.

3. Make periodic measurements or assessments of performance. This is more productive than providing one final assessment at the end of a project. Do not wait until the end to provide your feedback.

4. Provide ongoing feedback throughout a project or task so your people can adjust and course-correct as necessary to perform at the level you initially identified.

5. When providing feedback about performance that does not meet your expectations, focus on descriptive feedback rather than evaluative feedback. Describe what the person has done in light of your performance standards. Avoid using words that communicate good and bad.

6. Ensure that corrective action is taken as a result of your feedback. Get the person back on track. Make certain that the performance shortfall does not occur again.

When raters want you to decrease or do less of this behavior: Your raters are saying that you give them too much information, too much feedback. They may think you are communicating too often or provide them with too much detail. They may be tuning you out as a result. Provide them with more details when they request more details.

When raters see this behavior as a strength: Build on your strengths! Your raters are satisfied with the amount and frequency of your feedback. They know where you and they stand. They understand how their performance meets (or exceeds) your expectations.

Directional feedback is critical for action planning.

....

Example 2
Your assessment Competency-Theme is: Coaching
The item under this competency is: Provide feedback in a constructive manner.

Developmental suggestions for this item could include the following:

When raters want you to increase or do more of this behavior: Your rater groups feel that the feedback you give should be more constructive. It should not be criticism. It should not punish or blame them. There is a difference between constructive feedback, which is descriptive, and that which is evaluative.

Descriptive feedback

can facilitate behavior

change. Evaluative

feedback can facilitate

defensive behavior.

Descriptive feedback is the most powerful form of feedback because it describes the situation rather than judges the situation. Have you ever recorded your voice and then said to yourself, "I didn't know I spoke like that or that I pronounced that word like that?" The recorder only captures what you did. It does not critique your recording. There is no evaluation. For this reason, descriptive feedback more often than not leads to positive behavior change. It provides people with feedback that is difficult to argue with or avoid.

You can say how you feel — emotionally or physically—with descriptive feedback. You can use an "I-message," such as *"I feel frustrated or let down when you do not complete your work on time."*

When giving evaluative feedback to people, you may interject subjective comments, such as *"I thought your last presentation was really muddled and amateurish."* The other person's first response could be defensive. The person feels the need to defend or argue about what you said and what they believe they did.

You could have given descriptive feedback and have said, *"In your presentation you made point A, then moved to point C, and this made me confused."*

When raters want you to decrease or do less of this behavior: You may find that they are saying that the type of feedback you give is too constructive and diplomatic. They may not understand the message you are really trying to give. Use more descriptive feedback so folks will be able to see their behavior more clearly.

When raters see this behavior as a strength: The people who provided you with feedback said that your feedback is both constructive and useful to them. Build on this positive practice of yours!

Prescriptive Examples

Most Web-based application software does not allow you to provide directional feedback. Yet you can easily include a resource guide and provide prescriptive developmental ideas. For example, if one of the items on your assessment was "Allows you to finish speaking without interrupting," your resource guide and developmental suggestions could include something along these lines:

....

Example 1
Your assessment Competency-Theme is:
Communicating with Others
The item under this competency is: Allows you to finish speaking without interrupting.

Developmental suggestions for this item could include the following:

Effective communication is essential in today's world. Effective communicators are more influential with others. They are respected and trusted. How you communicate (e.g., how you listen, write, and speak) is as important as what you are trying to communicate. Are you talking too much? Provide the other person with airtime. If you talk too much or too long, it encourages less talking and interest on the part of the other person. Have you ever listened to someone who talked for a long time and who then asked you to comment on what (s)he said? Your typical reaction was probably very short. You probably forgot most of what the other person said. Of course, you may have tried to fake it by filling the air (that is, by talking too much yourself) in order to cover up what you missed. Consider these developmental suggestions to increase your effectiveness:

1. Be aware that some people have difficulty communicating. Provide them with ample time to respond to what you are saying. Do not get nervous because things suddenly go quiet.
2. Some people prefer to think before they speak. They prefer to formulate an idea and then communicate that idea. To you, their silence may represent a problem or

Include key learning points from your training programs.

perhaps silence makes you uncomfortable.

3. Do not assume that you know what a person is going to say before they say it.
4. Do not complete a thought or a sentence for someone else. You are interrupting and you are telling the other person that (s)he is not capable of expressing him or herself effectively, so you have to do it for him/her. It also tells people you are impatient!
5. Become an empathic listener. This is a non-critical stance towards the other person's ideas. The other person feels appreciated. They feel listened to. Empathic listening goes beyond the "I hear you" or "I can appreciate how you feel" statements. Empathic listeners say, "So you think that . . . " or "I can see how you are concerned about . . ." or "It seems that you . . ." or "You were really frustrated about that comment and you were about to ...." It demonstrates that you really understand what the person means and feels. It minimizes misunderstandings. It creates a more positive and productive exchange between you and the other person.

You could also include a brief description and registration information for your traditional or online training programs. Here are some possible program descriptions:

Developing Your Listening Skills
This two-day program will help you to improve your ability to listen to others. Learn the skills you need to understand what people say, read their nonverbal messages, and get others to want to listen to you. Learn how to apply these skills in a variety of business situations, such as interviews, business meetings, and negotiations.
Selected topics include:
1. Recognizing the benefits of improving personal listening skills.
2. Identifying the best practices for listening to yourself.
3. Matching the strategies for effectively listening to others with an example of each.

For more information or to register for this program, contact Yu Kno Whu at 555.952.7788.

Example 2
Your Competency-Theme is: Communicating with Others
The item under this competency is: Demonstrates patience (and attention) when listening to someone.

Developmental suggestions for this item could include the following:

Are you impatient? Do you tend to get anxious when the car ahead of you doesn't bolt from the stoplight as quickly as you think it should? Do you tend to question a person's heritage or lack thereof? Do you tend to get angry? Do you lose your temper? Do you tend to get uncomfortable when you have to wait in a checkout line when you are in a hurry? Do you find yourself saying things like, "By the time I explain this to her, I can complete it myself" or "I am patient but that person just doesn't seem to catch on quickly (i.e., as quickly as I would like)." Consider yourself impatient if you've responded positively to even some of these questions.

What is your hurry? Why are you so impatient? If you do not have time (or the patience) to listen to someone, why should they take the time to listen to you? Why should they be patient with you if you do not get something as quickly as they think you should?

As a starting point, consider these developmental suggestions to increase your effectiveness:

1. Resist the temptation to interrupt others.
2. Resist the temptation to interrupt and complete the thoughts of another person.
3. Become a more active listener. You could learn something new or gain new insights to an issue.
4. Think about how you react when people are not patient with you.

It is quite probable that one of your training programs will apply to multiple items in your survey. For example, a program entitled "Developing Your Listening Skills" could apply to both this and the previous item. You may also want to include space in your resource guide so participants can make notes.

For example, "*I can increase my effectiveness by . . .*"
Participants can print any page of the guide, make their
notes, and apply the recommendations in the guide to
their self-directed action plan(s).

....

Example 3
Your Competency-Theme is: Communicating with Others
The item under this competency is: Adjusts his/her
communication style to the situation, person.

Developmental suggestions for this item could include the
following:

Think about how you talk with people. Ask yourself how you
would respond if someone talked the same way to you. What
style of communication do you think you have? Do you adjust
how you speak to certain people or to groups of people?

Once you analyze how you typically speak to others, for
example, ask your team about your style and what you could
do differently to communicate more effectively in different
situations. For example, if you speak rapidly now (though you
may not think so), slow down. If you tend not to use gestures
when you speak, consider doing so. If you tend to talk in a
monotone, consider varying your tone a bit to emphasize
particular points. Conversely, if you are very animated when
you talk (from the point of view of others, of course), consider
toning it down. Your high level of excitement can cause
people to become a bit anxious around you. If you tend to
talk quickly, slow it down a bit.

Consider these other developmental suggestions to increase
your effectiveness as a starting point:

1. Do not interrupt!
2. Hear what the other person says. When listening, do not
   think about what you will say next.
3. Follow up with some people and ask them how you
   could say something more effectively.

4. Understand the other person's point of view before you explain your point of view. Summarize what you believe you heard. Make certain the other person agrees with your understanding.
5. Do not adjust your style by blaming, or by being accusatory, pejorative, or sarcastic.

The following training programs might assist participants receiving the above feedback:

Communication Skills
This two-day program will give employees the opportunity to improve their non-verbal, verbal, and visual delivery when communicating to a large or small group, or one-on-one.
Primary topics covered
1. Effective body language and use of the voice.
2. Correct breathing.
3. Control of stress to optimize delivery.
4. Essential communication skills to use in difficult situations.

Interpersonal Communication
This one-day course is designed to give you an understanding of the prime causes of poor communication and, more importantly, the skills required to minimize their impact.
Primary topics covered
1. Identifying the benefits of improving the effectiveness of interpersonal communication.
2. Identifying the benefit of being able to recognize and respond to the preferred communication styles of staff, colleagues, and clients.
3. Identifying the objectives for the aiming, encoding, and transmission stages of the communication process.

Communicate for Results
For many people, success in the workplace depends on their abilities to influence others to take a particular course of action. Consider this two-day training program.
Primary topics covered
1. Communicating with colleagues and coworkers.
2. Communicating with existing customers.
3. Communicating with your managers and directors.

Identify resources to help participants improve.

Example 4
Your Competency-Theme is: Developing Others
The item under this competency is: Provides you (others) with clear work priorities, realistic time lines for projects, tasks.

Developmental suggestions for this item could include the following:

You may have difficulty focusing your energies on a single task. You may prefer to be involved in multiple tasks and projects. You may have the tendency to jump from task to task. You may find it more interesting to work a little on one task, jump to another, then jump back to the first task and so on, before completing either task. You may have a short attention span. You may be bored with the task or project. You may not be committed to a task. Your feedback suggests you need to improve in this area. You need to commit yourself to doing what you need to do to make certain a task is completed within the agreed upon time line.

The best way to maintain focus on a project is to develop plans that will guide your actions in both the short and longer term. Identify the goal of the project. Identify the delivery date (deadline) and how successfully you are doing what needs to be done by certain checkpoints. Identify what needs to be done by whom (you and others). Identify your go/no-go decision points. Are there budgetary constraints? If so, what are they and how well are you operating within those guidelines? Have you delegated tasks that could be delegated to others? What additional resources will you need that you may (or may not) have planned for?

Consider these additional ideas to increase your effectiveness.

1. At the end of each week identify the exact time and effort you spent on a task or project. Did you accomplish what you said you intended to accomplish that week? If not, what will you need to do differently next week?
2. Plan to keep others informed on a weekly basis about your progress and any emerging issues or problems.
3. Channel your energies towards what you need to do "tomorrow," not what you did yesterday.

4. Listen to the excuses you are making for not maintaining a proper focus. Are you blaming others for this? What suggestions do they have for you?

Your organization may not have sufficient internal programs to cover all topics on your assessment. There may be Web-based programs that suffice. These programs may be free, allowing your employees to access them at any time. You may also need to contract with the vendor and create a hyperlink from your resource guide directly to their site and/or program.

Two Web-based programs might be as as folllows.

Managing Multiple Priorities
Rapid change, flatter structures, and cross-functional duties mean that individuals today must assume greater responsibility for managing their own tasks. To do that, employees need to know how to handle competing priorities; shift gears smoothly; and coordinate and negotiate responsibilities, schedules, and resources with others.
Topics covered
1. Identifying priorities.
2. Setting priorities.
3. Delegating.
4. Handling interruptions.
5. Clarifying expectations.

If you would like to register for this program, **click here** *<hyperlink to the program>. If you would like more information about this program,* **click here** *<e-mail link to the program coordinator>.*

Introduction to Project Management
This introductory course focuses on acquiring the basic skills and knowledge required for the planning and process of project management. This course delivers individual, organizational, business, and process skills for use in a project management setting.
Topics covered
1. Initiating a project.
2. Planning a project.
3. Reviewing issues with projects.
4. Learning project dynamics.
5. Identifying successful project ingredients.

6. Executing a project.
7. Controlling a project.
8. Managing risk.
9. Closing a project.

If you would like to register for this program, **click here** *<hyperlink to the program>. If you would like more information about this program,* **click here** *<e-mail link to the program coordinator>.*

Developmental ideas

may not require training.

You can make your guide as simple and straightforward as you want. For example, you can simply list a series of activities that participants can implement immediately.

Example 5
Your Competency-Theme is: Delegating to others
The item under this competency is: Knows what and when to delegate.

Developmental suggestions for this item could include the following:

Do you have too much to do and not enough time to do it? You can work faster. You can work longer hours. You can refuse to do it. Or you can delegate. Consider the following:

1. What tasks are you responsible for?
2. What must you retain (because of your title/position)?
3. What could you delegate if you wanted to?
4. What is preventing you from delegating that task to your employees now?
5. What do you intend to do to remove that barrier?
6. Accept the fact that your employees can do certain tasks as well as (or better than) you can.
7. Analyze your workload. Identify what you could delegate to get additional time to complete higher-level tasks.
8. Delegate tasks that build upon an employee's strengths.
9. Delegate tasks incrementally to allow employees to learn by doing and to take on more important issues over time.
10. When you fail to delegate you are telling employees that you do not trust them to do tasks effectively; that

you lack confidence in their abilities; that you are not interested in helping them expand their knowledge and areas of responsibility; that you are not interested in helping them reach their potential.

....

Example 6
Your Competency-Theme is: Delegating to Others
The item under this competency is: Assigns tasks to the most qualified employees.

Developmental suggestions for this item could include the following:

1. Who are your most productive employees and how do you know?
2. Who are your self-starters?
3. Who needs more guidance (initially) and throughout a project/task?
4. Match employees' strengths with work assignments.
5. Think of delegation as an onion. Provide employees with layers or segments of a task, rather than the entire task. As they perform, peel back another layer and provide them with additional responsibilities. Help them learn as they go. Coach them.
6. Provide employees with the training they need to succeed. You can do it yourself or have HR or other resources provide the training if you cannot or choose not to.
7. DPR! **Demonstrate** what you want done. Show employees the right way to do what you want done. Help them learn by **prompting** them through the process as they do it themselves. **Release** them to complete the task on their own when they can explain how something needs to be done to you or someone else.
8. Provide direction and assistance as needed. Do not hover. Do not micro-manage.
9. Ask your employees what they believe they will need to complete the task successfully.
10. Follow up on their progress on weekly basis. Reinforce what they are doing effectively. Coach them where improvement is needed.

Facilitate learning:

- **Demonstrate**

- **Prompt**

- **Release**

Notes:

Appendix Focus

Comparing electronic and paper processes; agendas for conducting feedback interpretation sessions; psychometric basics and their application to 360-degree feedback; norms and normative data; statistical terminology; ensuring long-term success; accountability for organizational success; organizational integration of 360-degree feedback; beyond woo-woo; planning for change.

- PERSPECTIVES
- DESIGNING IT
- DEVELOPING IT
- DEPLOYING IT
- DELIVERING IT

Comparing Media: Electronic versus Paper

W *We thought we had a very unique client in Asia. This was a large government agency that was impressed with our Web-based system. (Thank you.) They paid for our travel expenses and other costs. We, along with our CCi partner, made a dazzling presentation to the folks in personnel. We won the day and there were smiles all around. Well, almost. There was one person from IT (security) who reminded his fellow workers that employees were not allowed to access the Internet during working hours. He reminded them that because of the sensitive nature of their work, e-mail messages (especially those with attachments) from outside the organization were considered spam. They went someplace to be reviewed, deleted, and then, perhaps, forwarded. There could be the potential for viruses and other bad things. Any software would have to be brought into the organization, installed, and maintained by the IT folks. He also reminded everyone that the time and effort to do this would perhaps not be worth the time and effort (namely his). There was a lot of other work to do. I remember the profuse apologies by the folks from personnel, who were all very sorry for this and any inconvenience we may have experienced traveling all this way; there was also something about a "perhaps next time" and, oh by the way, farewell. I believe I remember smiling as we left the meeting. I know we left without the sale.*

Doubtless there will always be paper-based surveys. That said, you may want to compare paper and Web-based formats.

Accessibility issues: A Web-based system is not always practical. Employees may not have direct access to the Internet at work. They may be working in the field or on a drilling rig, for example. Many organizations do not have a room full of spare computers where employees can schedule time to complete surveys. Some organizations in some countries do not allow certain groups to access the Internet at all during working hours. As a result, direct reports or support personnel, for example, may not be able to complete the assessment. Advantage: paper.

Procrastination is not

limited to paper formats.

Competency issues: Not everyone is computer literate. That may sound a bit odd to you, but we hear from a wide range of organizations who tell us that many of their employees do not know how to use a computer, much less complete a Web-based assessment. Taking a few minutes to guide employees through a Web-based assessment does not sound like a major undertaking, yet it apparently is not worth the time and effort for some organizations. Sometimes we hear it is a language issue. Sometimes we hear it is the educational level that is the issue. Regardless of what they tell us, a Web-based format does not seem to be workable for the people we talk with in those organizations. Advantage: paper.

Personal issues: While many employees have a home computer, they may not want to share their personal e-mail and/or want to take their personal family time to complete a Web-based survey. Advantage: paper.

Procrastination issues: It wasn't too many years ago (the late 1990s in fact) that folks were debating the merits of paper surveys versus electronic formats. Yes, the electronic medium can collect the information faster, as long as people respond quicker. Until raters complete and submit their responses, however, there is not much difference between cyberspace and paper space when the speed of data collection is being discussed. Surprise! And raters can just as easily delete an e-mail notification message as they can toss a paper survey into the trash. Advantage: A draw.

Collusion issues: Some people dislike the 360-degree process because they fear raters will collude with one another and skew the results, aka "gang up" on a participant. That is an ongoing concern with paper surveys. It is almost impossible with a Web-based system that randomizes all items whenever any rater logs on to complete the assessment. Advantage: Web-based.

Deployment issues: You can deploy any Web-based assessment to anyone, from one to thousands, around the world at the same time. That is, instantly, within seconds. All you need is a name and e-mail address and access to the Internet. Simple! Of course, you can mail that same assessment to anyone, from one to thousands, around the world at the same time. When raters receive it is another matter. The cost of envelopes, postage, and personnel time is far more expensive and time consuming than with a Web-based assessment. Advantage: Web-based.

Delivery issues: You can send the results faster electronically than by truck or bus or plane or boat or hand delivery. Raters can receive your Web-based assessment at the same time, more or less. There is no postage with electronic data transfer. There are no customs forms or delays at customs when the results are sent across borders. You save time and money. Advantage: Web-based.

Data-compiling issues: As data is collected, Web-based software automatically links and compiles it to each participant more quickly than any hand-entered or scannable process can. There is no need for the administrator to sort through paper-based surveys and group them according to each participant or in a sequence required by a scanning program. Advantage: Web-based.

Real-time reporting: Inquiring minds want to know when they can see the results. Nothing much happens until raters complete and return their responses. With Web-based systems, when all or a statistically sufficient number of responses are returned, participants can see their results. Administrators can compile the results at the click of a button. Advantage: Web-based.

Security issues: Some folks fear their responses will be lost in cyber-space or somehow revealed to folks who should not have access to their responses. All paper surveys have some coding that identifies the participant and their respective raters. How else will a rater's responses be linked to the appropriate participant? Any paper survey must be handled (and therefore can be seen) by at least one other person, if only to remove it from the envelope and place it in a scanner for data entry. (You are not still using a hand-entry method, are you?) Could not that person peek at the responses? Web-based surveys are far more secure than paper surveys. Advantage: Web-based.

Time issues: Every assessment requires an amount of time to create, revise, and finalize it before being deployed. Once the assessment is finalized and ready to deploy, Web-based assessments typically consume much less time than paper surveys. With paper surveys you have to take into account the time and personnel needed to lay out the format. You need envelopes for distributing and returning the surveys to someone in the organization or to the external vendor. There is an inventory of surveys, instructions, and tracking forms to contend with as well. The time it takes for the person who will administer the feedback project, internal or external, needs to be taken into account. Excluding the time it takes to actually print all that needs to be printed, the average ratio of time needed to set up the survey, deploy it, track the status, follow up with raters who have not quite gotten around to completing it, send out a second survey to those who "lost it" or who somehow "never received it," and then deliver the feedback results to a group of n-10 participants is almost 5:1. That is, conservatively, it takes about 28 hours for a paper format compared to about 6 hours with a Web-based format. Advantage: Web-based.

Change issues: Web-based systems allow you to make changes to any assessment faster and easier than you can with paper-based assessments. You can make changes in real-time, conduct beta-tests, and make any final changes quickly, with less time and money. You can create a single assessment for your organization or create multiple assessments for any function, location, or demographic you need without having to worry about printing or inventory issues. Advantage: Web-based.

In short, electronic data collection is the standard now and will be for the foreseeable future. People are impatient and they want their results sooner rather than later. The folks who administer the feedback project want it to be quick and easy without the busy work often associated with paper-based surveys. Electronic data collection may have begun as an oddity or something novel, perhaps seen as just so much more e-commerce whiz-bang-woo-woo stuff. Today it is not. Compare both formats and select the format that works best for the person who will have to administer the 360-degree project and is most practical for your organization and your employees or customers.

Structured Feedback Workshops: Three Primary Agendas

We've always included a structured, facilitator-led feedback workshop for our clients. We continued this practice from the 1970s through the very early 1990s. Today, in this new century, many clients prefer a Web-based self-instructional format to an interpretative feedback workshop. There are advantages and disadvantages to any format. Nevertheless, there are clients who prefer the group setting. There are clients who prefer someone to guide their people through their data, respond to their questions, and provide them with the direction for creating self-directed action plans. We use any of the following agendas with clients, depending on their needs and requirements. Generally, all of our feedback workshops begin in the morning. All of our structured agendas follow the same format for the morning segment. The afternoon segment varies, again, depending on the needs and requirements of the client.

1. Feedback Workshop: Half-Day

A typical morning session could include the following . . .

- Introductions and objectives of the session.
- Identify the four (plus one) types of feedback participants could see in their feedback results.
- Guide participants through each reporting format and focus on how to interpret the data, as well as how that report will help them work more effectively with others.
- Share the group composite data for these participants.
- Guide participants through the action-planning process and have them create at least one such plan.
- Identify follow-up strategies for how participants can share their results with others using the CCi Surveys International follow-up discussion and coaching guide as their reference.
- Identify ongoing follow-up discussion and coaching sessions with participants' immediate bosses (and others if that is the client's expectation).

2. Feedback Workshop: Half-Day with Coaching
Conduct the morning session as outlined above, then . . .

Conduct one-on-one twenty- to thirty-minute coaching sessions with each participant to respond to any questions in private and to help them apply what they have learned from their feedback results. The purpose is to help participants with any concerns they have about their data and/or to provide them with suggestions for sharing their results with others, especially their bosses. These coaching sessions are mandatory for everyone. This avoids the stigma of having any one participant identified as having "problems" with his/her feedback. Participants sign up for a specific coaching session and return to work until the time of their session. This afternoon segment can roll over into the next day, depending on the number of participants and how much time you want to spend with each person.

3. Feedback Workshop: Full- or Multi-Day with Eight Options
Conduct the morning session as outlined above, then . . .

Option One: Create at least three subject-matter-expert (SME) discussion groups with those participants whose feedback identifies them as highly effective in those competencies identified as overall weaknesses in the group composite profile. The purpose is to identify what these SMEs do specifically that makes them highly effective. SMEs share their tips and suggestions, which can then be integrated into participants' self-directed action plans. Participants can move from discussion group to discussion group as they wish. Allocate sixty minutes for these discussion groups. Allocate another thirty minutes for a round-table debriefing that summarizes what each SME discussed and for additional suggestions from the consultant-facilitator. Just prior to the end of the day, create triads so participants identify what they intend to do differently as a result of their feedback, when they intend to share their data and with whom, etc.

Option Two: Create action-planning groups with participants who share the same developmental needs. The purpose is to identify what they could be doing differently to resolve these weaknesses. Allocate thirty- to forty-five minutes for this exercise. Include another thirty to forty-five minutes for a round-

Identify your subject-matter-experts.

table debriefing so each group can share what they discussed in their respective groups. Other participants along with the consultant-facilitator can provide their suggestions at this time.

Option Three: Review the group composite profile to identify strengths to build upon and areas of overall weakness. Create smaller discussion groups that link areas for overall development with the organization's strategic goals for the year. This exercise works especially well with a sales group, and helps participants understand the consequences of their actions on their customers in their respective territories. The discussion can also focus on how these developmental needs are affecting the overall performance and productivity of the sales unit/office/group. Members of each group discuss how they can resolve any of these weaknesses, and strategies are then shared with the entire group in a debriefing session. Each participant then creates at least one action plan that aligns with a strategic goal. Other action plans can be created for self-development as needed.

Option Four: Use the group composite profile to create a more effective team. Teams can be intact workgroups or executive-level teams or boards. All participants use their individualized data to identify what strengths and weaknesses they bring to the team. The primary purposes are to identify what the group does well as a group and how each participant can build upon these strengths to continue the success of the group. Participants create action plans that identify how they intend to resolve their individual weaknesses for both their self-development and the success of the group-team.

Option Five: Create group composite profiles for each department or functional area. Create discussion groups designed to identify specific solutions to these questions: How are these developmental needs blocking our departmental or organizational goals?; If we were to resolve these issues successfully, how would that improve our relationships with others (our clients, our personnel, our suppliers, etc.)?; If we do not resolve these weaknesses or developmental issues, what would be the consequences to us and to the organization?; What are the positive and negative consequences to us and to the organization (or to a client group, etc.) if we implement strategies to resolve these developmental needs OR if we

Modify application exercises to your organization.

choose not to implement any remedial strategies? (That is, what would happen if we did nothing?)

The organization can integrate the feedback results with its training programs. You can apply either of these options with training programs of two days or more.

Option Six: Complete the feedback interpretation segment on the morning of the first day. Devote the subsequent days to your training program, then return to the feedback results on the last day so participants can create their action plans. The feedback identifies the critical developmental areas to work on. The content in your training program can help them become successful, and more effective.

Option Seven: Conduct the feedback workshop on the morning of the first day, then conduct the training program in the afternoon of the first day and on the remaining days of your program. Use the afternoon of the last day of training for creating action plans and having participants identify what they have learned, what they intend to apply, and what they intend to do differently as a result of both their feedback and the organization's training. A variation of this format is to modularize training programs so that, depending on the overall group composite profile, trainers can drop or reduce the content for those areas where most or all participants are seen as highly effective, and use that time to focus on those modules where participants are not as effective. The overall time is the same. The organization simply shifts the focus from dumping all training content on the captive audience to providing a needs-driven focused approach to training.

Option Eight: This option is similar to option seven, except that prior to each content area in your program, instruct participants to return to their 360-degree feedback results. They review only that set of data that pertains to what you are about to cover. That is, if your first training module is about problem solving and decision making, participants review the data for that competency. They identify which specific behaviors they need to develop and which they can build upon because they are strengths. In this option, you return to the feedback throughout your training program. For example:

360-DEGREE FEEDBACK WITH MULTI-DAY TRAINING PROGRAMS		
DAY ONE: EARLY MORNING	**BREAK**	**DAY ONE: LATE MORNING AND AFTERNOON**
• Orientation to your program. • Rules and riot control. • Conduct feedback interpretation session so participants understand how to interpret their data and learn their strengths and developmental needs.	**FEEDING TIME**	• Prior to your first content area, participants review their feedback results for the content area you are about to cover in your program. • Deliver your content module for that area, e.g., Communication Skills. • Link the behaviors and practices in the 360-degree survey to the content in your traning program.

360-DEGREE FEEDBACK WITH MULTI-DAY TRAINING PROGRAMS		
DAY TWO AND FOLLOWING	**BREAK**	**LAST DAY OF PROGRAM**
• Continue with each module in your training program after participants review their feedback results for that content area. • As with the prior afternoon, deliver each content module for the different content areas in your program. • Link the behaviors and practices in the feedback survey with the content in your training program.	**FEEDING TIME**	• Complete your last content area. • Return to the 360 results and have participants create self-directed action plans that identify what area(s) they intend to develop and what they intend to do differently as a result of their feedback and your program content.

One of our multinational clients had a somewhat novel approach to integrating the 360-degree process with its six-day leadership development program. Participants received their personalized feedback profiles on Thursday. We provided self-instructional guides so they could understand their results. They arrived off-site, usually at a rather nice resort, by late Sunday afternoon just prior to the welcome and social hour and dinner. After dinner the consultants hired by the client went over the agenda, objectives, learning outcomes, and instructions; created the leadership teams; and identified some of the activities in the program. The next morning the program began at 6:30 with breakfast and their first working session. Participants were called upon to explain each of the reporting formats in their feedback profiles. Instructors guided them. When someone had a question, another participant was called upon to explain it. The client's expectations were simple: these folks make the big bucks. They can learn how to interpret their results on their own time. During the training program they were expected to apply what they learned from their results and develop a maximum of three action plans based on those results. The sessions were full-day affairs, with additional team activities at night, typically lasting tuntil 10:00 p.m. Participants returned to *their feedback at the start of each new content area, reviewed their data, then were led through the training content by the consultants-instructors. Wednesday afternoon and evening was play time. Otherwise, the program was full with lectures, application exercises, team activities, a little team competition, and on the last day, action planning. After participants completed their action plans, they were required to stand and identify what they intended to do differently as a result of their feedback, what aspects of the training program they would include in those action plans, who they planned to share their feedback with and when, and how often they intended to follow up with their boss or the rater groups included in the action plans. Other participants and the consultants-instructors offered suggestions for each action plan as needed. Participants were held accountable for their actions and action plans. This client has been and continues to be number one or two in their multiple businesses.*

Psychometrics: An Overview

Is your survey statistically valid and reliable? And how do you know? And do you care about reliability and validity? Every survey should be well written, but not every survey needs to be statistically sound. For example, if your 360-degree assessment is *only* for self-awareness with no accountability for applying the feedback results, then maybe you do not need it. Conversely, if you use the feedback to hire or to promote people or provide them with compensation based on those results, you may want to look more closely at the statistical worth of your instrument.

Did you change the assessment? When you change any item on a generic assessment, that assessment is no longer the same, statistically. Any assessment you customize or tailor to your organization is a "new" assessment. It does not have comparative reliability or validity, except perhaps face validity. If you want to talk about higher levels of validity, for example, you will need to deploy the survey, collect data from a statistically representative sample, and conduct a procedure called factor analysis.

In all cases, you need to have a database of responses by people who have taken the assessment. If you create a custom survey and deploy it to the first group of people, there is no validation or reliability that you can speak of (again, except perhaps face validity). When multiple groups have completed your custom assessment and you have created a database of their responses of at least a few hundred people, then you can move to a more formal analysis of your survey. Varied analytical techniques can be used to establish whether an instrument is reliable or valid.

Psychometrics and 360-Degree Assessments

Applying a more rigorous approach to the development of a 360-degree assessment is a clear positive. Creating performance-based 360-degree assessments that focus on what people do on the job is relevant to participants. Another positive. The trend towards a more structured 360 process is welcomed. The slap-dash-get-it-done approach is a waste of time and money. It is not in the interests of the participants nor the organization.

Applying psychometrics to the 360 process can also be positive. Yet the majority of statistical analyses have been conducted on psychological tests, IQ tests, style preference instruments, career and vocational interest batteries, and, well, tests in general. These tests and batteries incorporate a single response scale or a forced choice scale. These tests and batteries and instruments do not focus on performance. They do not focus on what folks do on their job. They focus on what folks prefer to do or what they know.

A performance-based 360-degree assessment is neither a test nor a measure of knowledge. There are no right or wrong answers. There are no (or very few) psychometrics on dual-scale 360 assessments. Some psychometric properties may not lend themselves to 360 with their multi-rater groups. Therefore, to apply current standards for psychometric analysis may not be as applicable to performance-based 360 as some folks might suggest. Yet this is what is happening in an effort to judge the statistical worth of a 360-degree assessment.

For example, the critical and core tenant of performance-based 360-degree assessments (and all 360 assessments for that matter) is the observation of specific behaviors and practices performed by the participant. Different rater groups see the participant differently and in different situations depending on their relationship to the participant. One rater group might see the participant as highly effective in a behavior, while another does not. One rater within a rater group can see the participant as highly effective with respect to a behavior, while another rater does not. From a psychometric point of view, this cannot be a good thing. From a 360-degree point of view, it is a good and valuable insight. It is what 360-degree assessment is all about—multiple perspectives and multiple observations and multiple situations and multiple assessments of behavior. Identifying gaps or deltas between and among rater groups and raters within those groups is the cornerstone of the 360-degree feedback process.

These deltas, if they are in the feedback results, can easily identify where (by specific behaviors) and with whom (not by individual name, but rather by rater group) the participant is highly effective and where and with whom they are not. This contextual delta between and among raters in comparison to the participant's self-reported data is a positive. This contextual delta can help shatter the belief that there is a best way to lead and manage. It can help shatter the notion that there is one best way to do anything!

Psychometric properties for tests and style preferences and interest batteries are relevant. There can be a statistically distinct set of traits or descriptors or factors that support a career choice or the predictive ability of a person to succeed in a given function or position, for example. Conducting a data analysis technique on a 360-degree assessment, such as factor analysis, is relevant and important, especially when the results of that assessment will be used for higher-level applications, i.e., higher than self-awareness. Use caution when applying the same psychometric properties and standards and guidelines used for test construction to a multi-rater feedback process, such as 360. That said, here are some psychometric properties you may want to become familiar with as they are commonly used and as they relate to 360.

The purpose of this section is not to discount the standards or methodologies associated with different psychometric properties. Rather, I include this section to inform and caution the reader about automatically applying these psychometrics to the 360 process. Discretion is advised.

I will focus on reliability and validity. We need to talk about reliability before we can talk about validity. The basics of reliability include internal consistency, inter-rater consistency, and test-retest.

Reliability

Reliability refers to individual score consistency across repeated administrations. It refers to the degree to which the rating scales measure the dimensions, domains, or competencies consistently. Reliability is the freedom from measurement error; it is the stability, repeatability, consistency, or comparability. Reliability is usually a question of how much confidence can be placed in the accuracy of the ratings overall. Reliability can help answer the questions, "Does the assessment method hold up over time?" and "Does it hold up across different raters or groups of raters at the same time?" One way to determine the level of reliability is to correlate the data of the same person over time or across rater groups.

Inter-rater reliability measures the extent to which different raters (or rater groups) agree the participant is performing at the same relative level, for example. **Intra-rater reliability** measures the extent to which different raters within the same rater group agree the participant is performing at the same relative level. **Inter-rater reliability** would be important to you if you wanted to ascertain the extent to which all (or most) rater groups assessed the participant consistently. For example, did each rater group, the boss, direct reports, and peers, see the participant as highly effective (or not). **Intra-rater reliability** would be important to you if you wanted to know whether all raters within a specific rater group see the participant as highly effective (or not). That is, if there are four raters in the rater group labeled "Direct Reports" and they all have worked with the participant for about the same length of time, or more critically, have observed the participant's behavior for a reasonable amount of time, **intra-rater reliability** suggests that all four should see the participant at the same level of effectiveness or ineffectiveness or they should all be satisfied or equally dissatisfied with the participant's behavior.

Donald L. Whaley

published *Psychological Testing and the Philosophy of Measurement* in 1973.

Behaviordelia, Inc.

Both of these psychometric standards do not apply so neatly to 360-degree assessments. And they do not apply to dual-response scale 360-degree assessments that provide directional feedback to the participant. This directional feedback works against this psychometric. It can be common, indeed quite common, for some raters to see the participant as highly effective for a given behavior or practice; for other raters to recommend the participant do more of that behavior; and for still other raters to recommend the participant do less of that behavior to become more effective. This **intra-rater inconsistency** occurs because each rater has different expectations of the participant. Psychometrics can get a tad sticky here. A participant can understand and benefit from the fact that not all raters within that rater group think alike. They are individuals who have different needs. Some need the participant to do more of the behavior, while others require less of that behavior. Likewise, the participant could be highly effective or influential with one rater group, but not another. Both **inter-** and **intra-rater reliability** can be relevant for self-directed action planning.

Do you have two or more kiddies? Do they all think and act the same? Do some need more help and guidance than the others? Do you exercise your parental duties at the same level or to the same degree to each? You really don't. The analogy fits. Different kiddies need different levels of attention and support from you. Different direct reports (and probably everyone else) need different levels of attention and coaching and motivation and guidance and reinforcement from their bosses. Intra-rater consistency can identify that those differences exist with a rater group.

Raters may not see the participant in the same light as other raters in that rater group for several reasons. Raters respond to the items in an instrument based on their own perceptions and interactions with the participant. Contrary to popular belief, raters do not "gang up" on a particular person nor collaborate their responses to the extent that some people want to believe. And with some Web-based software systems, such as CCi Direct-Connect®, that is pretty much impossible. Second, most participants do not behave exactly the same with each person with whom they interact. Therefore, in the case of direct reports, some may be loosely managed (for whatever reason), others may be micro-managed (for whatever reason), and still others may be ignored or managed only when they screw something up.

Psychometricians could see a low score as indicating low **inter-rater** or **intra-rater reliability**. This would not be a good thing, normally. This could be all good for a 360-degree assessment because it can identify different perspectives and expectations. It can clearly indicate that not all direct reports, for example, are equal with respect to what they need from the participant. The same can be said of one's peers and internal or external customers. Feedback that flags inter- and intra-group discrepancies helps participants understand that they may be managing or interacting with people differently, with less-than-effective results. It can help participants understand that there is no one best way to manage or influence people. It can help participants understand the consequences of their behaviors within a specific group of raters and across all rater groups.

Internal consistency identifies the extent to which there is homogeneity within the scales of an assessment. Scales here are not single or dual BARS or numeric scales or multi-guess options. Rather scales as defined in psychometrics are the theme or competency labels. "Delegation" is a scale. "Problem Solving" is a scale. Scales include items and, in the case of a performance-based 360-dergee assessment, these items are written as observable behaviors and practices. Internal consistency answers the question, "Do the items listed for delegation measure delegation?"

The psychometrician would look for consistency across the items in that scale. Is the participant effective (or ineffective) across all items? The thinking is that if the participant is effective on one item, (s)he should be effective on all the other items. Sounds logical and tidy. Sounds pretty cut and dried. Sounds pretty unrealistic and messy when applied to the 360-degree process and is not as relevant to the results. The participant can be highly effective in some areas (items) for a competency, but ineffective in other areas.

As I mentioned, multiple rater groups and multiple raters in any one rater group could see the participant as effectively performing the same behavior and/or all other behaviors in that scale. If so, we could say there is internal consistency. In reality, each rater and each rater group as a whole could have different expectations for that participant as the rater interacts with the participant. Each rater could observe the participant under different circumstances, different situations. The rater's style can affect what they want and need from the participant. For example, extrovert-type people tend to be more vocal, need and expect more attention, and may need more verbal reinforcement from the participant. Introvert-type folks do not need as much attention; they typically do not ask nor expect to receive as much verbal reinforcement. In this example, intra-rater inconsistency would be expected. Again, this *inconsistency* is positive in a 360-degree assessment. It is reality. It can clearly identify what the participant can build upon when the behavior is a strength, and what to develop and in what direction (do more, do less) when it is a weakness. The application of the feedback results helps create more focused self-directed action plans.

Participants base their action plans on specific behaviors, not on a scale, unless the behaviors within that entire scale (or almost all of the items within that scale) have been identified as weaknesses and, as a result, the participant is seen as highly ineffective for that entire scale.

Test-retest compares a rater's assessment over a relatively short time. It measures the degree to which results from the same or different raters are stable or consistent from one assessment point to the next. This consistency should occur as long as the participant did not do anything differently during this short time frame. That is, the participant did not have any special training or coaching or mentoring during this time frame. And even if the participant did, additional time would be needed for raters to see the results of that training or coaching or mentoring. This short time-frame standard is irrelevant to the 360-degree process. Raters log on to complete their feedback responses. Yes, they can exit and enter as much as they want. However, the administrator has set a time line for all raters to submit their responses. That time line is identified in days or weeks, not months!

A rater completes one assessment on one participant once in this time frame. A rater may complete multiple assessments on multiple participants. Yet all raters provide their responses in a relatively tight time frame, e.g., from one to three weeks, depending on how much time you allow raters to complete their responses and when you choose to close the survey.

Raters can complete two assessments on the same participant when doing pre-post assessments, yet pre-post assessments do not occur in a short period of time. The generally recommended time frame between each pre-post assessment is from six to twelve months. Neither does test-retest reliability apply to pre-post assessments as cleanly as one would hope.

Pre-post assessments can identify progress and the effectiveness (or ineffectiveness) of changes the participant made as a result of taking the initiative to implement some of the ideas and techniques learned from training programs, coaching, or a mentoring intervention. The results could be dramatically different between the pre-post results. That could be a good thing, especially if the participant made changes that resolved a developmental challenge. As a result, it would be a given that raters' responses for the pre-assessment would be different than their responses for the post-assessment.

So where does this psychometric fit? All is not lost. Test-retest has greater relevancy when applied to your beta testing or pilot programs for your newly created 360-degree assessment. This psychometric can uncover a wide range of rater responses indicating poor design and construction. The layout on the screen may be confusing to raters. Poor instructions may contribute to its unreliability. The items may be ambiguous. An item may identify multiple issues rather than one behavior or practice. The items may be written with double negatives, thus confusing some raters. You can conduct a beta test and revise your assessment accordingly. You can then beta test again to identify the extent to which your revisions have resolved any rater problems or points of confusion. It is far better to beta test multiple times if necessary, rather than unleash a poorly constructed assessment on folks, especially if some of those folks are external to your organization, i.e., your customers! Use test-retest for measuring the effectiveness of how you developed your assessment.

Reliability Does Not Mean Valid

When you go to the doctor's for an exam, a nurse typically weighs you as you arrive off the street (minus your parka and car keys and cell phone and PDA and portable computer and attaché case, etc.). The nurse then records your weight. Let's assume the scale misrepresents your weight, adding ten pounds. And let's say you do not realize that it was adding these extra ten pounds. You step on that scale again, with the same clothing and see no real gain or loss in your weight. The scale is consistent (i.e., reliable), but the inference about how much you really weigh is not correct (i.e., not valid).

Thus your assessment can be reliable and provide a person with an effectiveness score, for example. Yet is it valid, i.e., does that score really represent that person's true effectiveness or ineffectiveness? It is easy to rationalize here. Let's return to our weight example. Suppose that the scale indicated that your weight was ten pounds less. And stepping on and off the scale, with the same clothing on, the reading measured these ten fewer pounds. As the proud owner of that lower poundage, would you be apt to call the ten pounds valid or invalid? Sometimes when data is in our favor we tend to side with the notion that it is valid because that is what we hoped the assessment or measure would show.

An instrument that is not reliable will also not be valid. An instrument that is reliable may not be valid.

Validity

What is your primary use for your 360-degree assessment? What does the feedback tell the participant? What can you infer from the scores? Stop! Stop focusing on the score of any item or theme (or scale). Regardless of the score, if a rater group sees a participant as ineffective for a specific behavior, then the participant may need to consider it for his/her action planning effort. Stop using 360-degree results as the sole basis for promotions or demotions or compensation or termination or any-tion! Use the results as one more snapshot of a participant's performance.

Validation may hold today, but perhaps won't tomorrow and certainly won't forever. Validity is an ongoing process. Validity can change as your target population changes. Some general issues for validation include the following:

• Does your 360-degree assessment measure what it says it measures, e.g., leadership or sales effectiveness or emotional intelligence?

- If the 360-degree assessment does indeed measure what it says it measures, are those behaviors and practices relevant to key aspects of the target population's job behavior? That is, if your 360-degree assessment measures personal integrity, is that important and/or relevant to a participant's leadership of others?
- Can the results serve as a catalyst for change? If your items are relevant and if they are observable and measurable, they should enable participants to create self-directed action plans. And when they are implemented, can participants change as a result of their ability to change from what they learned in a training program, through coaching and/or mentoring? Given their feedback, their ability to learn how to do things differently, and their willingness to do so, can you correlate those activities and interventions to behavior change by the participant?

Are you measuring what you want to measure?

So What Is Validity?

Validity is a measure of the usefulness of a procedure, technique, or device. "To what extent are we measuring what we want to measure?" One validates not a measuring tool, such as a 360-degree feedback instrument, but rather some use or application to which the instrument is designed for, e.g., leadership, team building. "*How credible is the assessment on the part of the raters?*" or "*Do the questions and items on the instrument appear to measure a construct called Delegation or Motivation or Problem Solving?*" There are different ways to talk about validity. Face validity is what most people think about when they toss around a question like, "Is it valid?"

Face validity is subjective in that there are no predetermined content domains with which to compare items. It relies on the judgments about whether the items in the instrument *look like* they measure what they are supposed to measure. Some people believe that creating an instrument is not a big deal. They create one from their experience as, say, when they were a salesperson managing a territory: "*Here is what I did as a salesperson, therefore here is what a survey (the behaviors and practices) for our salespeople should look like.*" People create surveys from the premise that, logically, the items they want to include to measure a theme called "Handling Resistance" *seem* *like* behaviors that can be called "Handling Resistance."

A survey is said to be valid when the person who created the survey (or a researcher) comes to the conclusion that the survey measures what (s)he says it was designed to measure. They have the experience, therefore the instrument they created or contributed to *must* be valid. As a result, you will hear people typically say the instrument has *face validity*. That is, it seems to measure what designers said it would measure based upon the face value of the items that comprise the instrument. This is the simplest (and least rigorous) form of validation.

"Is this instrument valid?" As stated, the question cannot be answered without first knowing for what purpose the validity is meant to apply. With respect to psychometrics, reliability needs to be established first before one can say the instrument is valid. There are other types of validation to be aware of.

Construct validity of an assessment is the extent to which the assessment may be said to measure a theoretical construct or trait or behavior or scale. It is the degree to which the people being assessed posses the behaviors or constructs presumed to be reflected in the assessment. It derives from established interrelationships among behavioral measures. Evidence of construct validity is not found in a single study; rather, judgments of construct validity are based upon an accumulation of research results. It is the cumulative support or evidence that an instrument is valid.

This type of validity identifies the extent to which the instrument measures what it is intended to measure when you have no specific criteria. For example, you may not be able to measure a concept like stress, but you can measure people's reactions to it or their attitudes towards it or how they perform under *stressful* conditions, and you can compare those results with results from another instrument, or with interviews, or observations, or other tests and inferences. You establish construct validity by generalizing from specifics.

Content validity involves professional judgments about the relevance of the instrument's content of a particular behavioral domain. Do the items adequately sample the domain or theme or competency? That is, to what extent does the instrument sufficiently cover the competency (scale). Some assessments only have one or two questions for, say, the competency categories "Communication" and "Leadership." This survey would not have content validity. There are insufficient items to cover that competency. I recommend that you include at least five items per competency.

Concurrent or predictive validity measures the extent to which instrument scores are related to current or future measures of external criteria. When the external criterion provides an indicator relevant to present functioning, the findings are supportive of concurrent validity. When those same criteria provide evidence relevant to future performance, we say the instrument has predictive validity.

Criterion referenced validity involves inferences about instrument scores. This type of validity has to do with how well such scores correlate with existing or future attitudes or behaviors. Do they predict something? For example, organizations that use assessment centers to predict future managerial success are concerned about the criterion referenced validity of the assessment procedure. These later two factors are a bit dicey with respect to 360-degree assessments. It could well be that a person who is highly effective today (pre-assessment) should be identified as highly effective tomorrow in a post-assessment. Likewise, if a participant is highly ineffective in some behaviors or competencies and they did not do anything differently to improve, we could *predict* that they will be ineffective tomorrow. Prediction is, by and large, the world of assessment centers. The 360-degree process is not (officially) in that business.

Discriminate validity is concerned with the ability of the instrument to discriminate and differentiate among the performances of people being evaluated. Can raters make their assessments based upon their experiences with the participant? This is a given with 360-degree assessments. Participants select (or certainly should select) raters who know them well and whose feedback they value. If there is variance in the feedback for participants within and among different rater groups or functions within the organization, then it can be said that the instrument is able to measure differences in observable behavior between and among participants.

Norms and Behavior Change

What are *norms*? A norm is the average score of all people who have taken a specific 360-degree assessment (or any other assessment survey for that matter). It can also represent the average score of a specific *norm group* or target population. A norm group is a target population, say managerial personnel, stored in a database (yours or the vendor's). If you can access this norm group you can compare your folks with those folks (or the folks in the norm group). That is, you can compare that normative data with your folks. However, this type of norm does not represent excellence. It does not necessarily represent what your target performance should be. It is not a paradigm for excellence. It is an average score. Again, think of that C from your days in college. C = excellence? No dean's list here!

Normative data is mistakenly seen as the paradigm or the standard to strive for. It is not, though the underlying assumption is that this score is what your folks should strive for. Some see the score as a best practice or a target. Well, the item, the behavior, may be a best practice and something to include in your change efforts, but the score is not a best practice by any stretch of the imagination. It represents mediocrity. Think about it. Do you want your folks to strive for mediocrity? If so, fine. It's your organization.

Norms do not necessarily represent a level of exceptional performance. They are not paradigms for excellence. Norms can help you strive for mediocrity, however. And sometimes when you aim for mediocrity, you actually realize it.

Why We Like Norms

How important are national or industry norms to you? They can be a guide or baseline. It is typical for people to want to know how they stack up to someone else or some other organization.

If you value comparing yourself to industry norms, keep the following in mind.

- Consider the folks who you will compare your folks to.
- If you process the data internally, you will *not* have access to data outside your organization.
- You could purchase a database to get the information against which to benchmark your employees, but why?
- How old is the data?
- You may be able to compare your first line supervisors with

other first line supervisors from your SIC (Standard Industrial Classification), but if you are going to benchmark, you need to know how effective the people in that database really are.

Norm addicts, beware! You may not know who is in the database. You can ask, of course! Yes, you can know gender and titles and functions and types of industries and educational levels and how long people have been on the planet. Some vendors create and maintain databases that can sort information demographically, such as information about supervisors who have worked with an organization for two to three years, about middle managers who have experience in marketing and sales. That could work. However, what you do not know is whether the people in the database represent the best employees, average employees, or simply those employees who fit the demographic (e.g., who have worked with the organization for two to three years and at one time were thought to be breathing). You do not know their levels of competence. As a result, the database for this normative data set, for example, could include folks who range from Mensa member to village idiot, from highly motivated and effective to catatonic and mentally retired.

But, hey, people like to compare. We like to compare our cholesterol levels with those of others. We like to know that we are at the top of the economic scale. We may not want to know that we are not. We complete those simple ten-item questionnaires we see in the newspaper to compare our social drinking or anger management or time management or conflict resolution habits. What do we do with that information? For most people, the answer is not much, other than to turn to the next page in the paper or periodical.

One problem with norms is that the focus is on a score and not necessarily the behavior. Think about your last discussion with such norms. Did you focus on whether they had a 3.4 and you had a 3.6? Or did you focus instead on the actual wording of the item? Did you overly analyze the significance of a .02 delta between the scores or the actual wording for that behavior? Purge your mind of scores! Focus on the behavior and the direction for change. To become more effective, should participants do more, do less, or build on current strengths for that specific behavior or practice to work more effectively with others?

Focus on the behavior, not the score.

Reactions to Norms

Focusing on norms can be a very convenient way to avoid taking responsibility for implementing needed change. One purpose of 360-degree feedback is that it can act as a catalyst for implementing needed change. However, when comparing their feedback to a national norm, people do funny things. If they are above the norm, they feel change is not needed. *I am better than others.* When they are at the same level, they feel change is not needed. *I am doing what everyone else is doing.* The real fun occurs when they score below the norm, as in below average. Defensive rationalization tends to take charge. People attack the survey. *Who created this assessment? How relevant are the questions to what I really do? Is this a valid survey? Is the data reliable?* People tend to look for excuses rather than expend the energy to become more effective or more competitive or to become more influential with others. In the end, all this sound and fury amounts to nothing more than if one were sitting in a rocking chair: There is the appearance of movement, but no forward progress.

Underlying all of this is your assumption about why you think you need to compare your employees with those from other organizations in the first place. If you believe your organization is unique, why would you want to compare your unique organization with organizations that are not as unique? And if you believe that the normative database is chock-full of unique organizations, then what is so unique about your organization? The discussion becomes a bit circular. Many organizations that are number one or two in their markets do not use national norms for comparative purposes. What would be the point?

Alternative to National Norms

One alternative to using national or industry norms is to create your own normative database about the people within your company. Create data that is self-norming to your targeted populations. Segregate the data of your best performing employees from that of your least effective. Identify your own critical behaviors and practices for all employees and for specific functional units.

Your software (or the vendor's) may allow you to compare your group of managers with, say, other managers within your organization who have taken the same instrument. Of course, if you have a proprietary assessment, you cannot do this with any externals because they have not completed your instrument. (Yours is a proprietary and custom assessment, remember?) The software may allow you to compare the current group of participants with (a) all other employees who have completed your assessment; and/or (b) those employees who are in the same demographic as the current group, i.e., first line supervisors, or women, or folks who have been with the company for more than ten years, and so on.

Statistical Terms for Party-Time Fun

There are some other statistical terms and psychometrics you may want to explore on your own. Here are some that you may find fun.

Assessment Instrument	The means, electronic, paper, or face-to-face, an organization uses to capture observations and knowledge. It is a structured format for gathering observations or knowledge from tests, examinations, questionnaires, surveys, and other sources for the purpose of drawing inferences about characteristics of people, objects, products, services, or programs for a specified purpose.
Authoring System	Computer programs that allow users to author and edit items, instructions, rating scales, e-mail messages, and other components.
Chi-Square or "Goodness of Fit"	A test to see if the observed frequencies of occurrence are significantly different (statistically) from the expected frequencies of occurrence.
Composite Profiles	The aggregated feedback results from at least five participants. Composites can identify collective strengths and developmental needs for any demographic you choose. Also called group profiles, demographic profiles, roll-ups, or training needs analysis profiles.
Diagnostic Assessment	Any assessment instrument can be a diagnostic assessment. Assessments are diagnosed (or their data analyzed) to identify training and development needs for any one individual or groups of individuals; for determining prior knowledge of specified content areas; for comparing pre-post feedback; for measuring the extent to which interventions such as coaching, mentoring, or training have been effective.

Factor Analysis (Explains the Correlations or Co-Variances Among a Set of Variables)

This is a key data analysis technique that identifies the extent to which each item on an assessment instrument loads or correlates with a particular theme or competency. Factor analysis can identify the quantitative evidence that an instrument includes those behaviors and practices that effectively measure each competency. It can identify the extent to which the items you include for "Delegation," for example, actually pertain to "Delegation."

Field Test

Also referred to as a beta test or pilot test, this is a test deployment of an assessment to check for a wide range of issues, such as the readability of instructions and items, the ease of access and exit by raters, the follow-up reminder messages to outstanding raters, the compilation and reporting of the test data. Field tests are administered to one or more individuals or one or more work groups.

Formative Feedback

Also referred to as prescriptive feedback and has as a key component a series of set developmental tips, techniques, strategies for helping 360-degree participants resolve (or reduce) weaknesses identified in their feedback. Each item in the assessment has its own canned prescriptions for development.

Frequency Analysis

Frequency data measure the number of instances or the frequency that a particular item, behavior, or practice was identified as a strength or weakness by rater groups who were asked to provide feedback on the assessment.

Item

A word, phrase, question, choice, or sentence that describes some aspect of a behavior, practice, skill, performance, or personal characteristic.

Item Analysis

Also referred to as detailed item analysis, it is the process of analyzing feedback results by each individual item (as compared to the theme or competency label). Participants typically create action plans by item.

Item Bank

A library of questions, behaviors, and practices that authors can access to create different assessments.

Likert Scale

A method incorporated into rating scales to prompt raters or respondents to express their opinion or observations on the item or statement presented. Likert scales are typically four-to-five point scales that include behavioral anchors, such as "Strongly Agree" to "Strongly Disagree;" or "Almost Always" to "Almost Never."

Measures of Skewness

Identifies whether the data is symmetrically distributed (as in a bell curve) or asymmetrically distributed (as in negatively skewed to the left or positively skewed to the right). Include frequency of distribution or response distribution columns in your reporting format and you will easily see the extent to which the data is skewed.

Measure of Position	This identifies where the data is concentrated. **Mean** is the mathematical average of the data. You obtain the mean by adding all the scores for a specific item or theme and dividing by the total number of people who responded to that item or the total number of items within that theme, for example.
	Median is the middle point in a data set. That is, 50 percent of the data is above the median and 50 percent is below it. If you have nine values or a string of 9 scores, the fifth value will be your median score.
	Mode is the most common data point found in the data set. That is, if "5" is the mode we can say that "5" was the response, the data point most often found in your data set. If you have a five-point response scale and if most raters responded with a "4" then the mode would be "4."
Measures of Variability	These identify the spread or distribution of the data set. **Range** is the difference between the largest and smallest observations in the data set.
	Variance (a zero variance) means that all the data points are the same. The more spread out the data points, the higher the variance.
	Standard deviation (the larger the standard deviation) identifies how much variation there is in the data set. The greater that variation, the greater the spread of responses or data points.
Normal Distribution	A bell curve. The shape of the curve identifies the responses or range of scores. Typically, most responses or raters center around the mean, with fewer people at either end of the curve.
Raters	The people who provided (or who were asked to provide) feedback.
Rater Groups	A collection of people with a common thread—i.e., direct reports, peers, or a functional group—that provided responses (or who were asked to provide responses) to items on your instrument.
Reference Population	Also referred to as the target population or demographic population, it identifies and includes the population of participants represented by the data or feedback results. The population can include any demographic defined in terms of gender, age, title, location, business unit, educational level, or other characteristics.

Self Norms	Also referred to as local norms, they are data based upon a specific and limited population. Self norms apply to a specific organization, locale, institution, department, or business unit. They are not industry or national norms.
Standard Deviation	Spread or variation. This is the square root of the variance among responses. It identifies how much variance a set of responses or scores deviates from the mean.
Statistical Significance	This indicates the existence of a difference or that a relationship exists. When a statistic is significant, you can be sure your statistic is reliable. It doesn't mean that this finding is important. Sample size affects whether the difference is important or not. With a large population or n count (n=number of people who returned a completed questionnaire or completed a specific item) small differences will be identified as significant. That is, the difference is real; it was not a fluke. It does not mean the difference is important, however. Once a difference is detected you may want to evaluate its strength. You can do that with either a one-tailed or a two-tailed significance test.
t-test	The t-test assesses the extent to which different groups are statistically different from each other. A t-test compares the means of two groups of observation to see if they are equal (and to see what differentiates one group from another). You could compare the results of men to women, or of managers from one location to another, or any other demographic comparisons. You could identify what behaviors separate your super performers from your mediocre performers.
Total N	Everyone who was sent a survey. Total N can include all of the raters who were asked to assess a particular person on a 360-degree instrument. It can include all employees from a specific function or location, for example.
Valid N	People who actually responded. Valid n is more significant than total n. Valid n identifies how many raters responded to a specific item out of the total n. For example, if 100 employees were asked to complete a survey and only 40 actually completed and returned it, your valid n would equal 40. Or 40 percent of your employees completed the survey, while 60 percent did not.
Weighted Responses	A method of scoring an assessment in which more (or less) points are given for a correct response (test items) or for a specific rater group (feedback from the boss).

How to Ensure Long-Term Success

Issues for Design

What is the purpose?

Is your feedback project to be used for self-awareness or self-development? Is it for career development or succession planning? Will the results be linked to your performance management process? Are you interested in employee opinions about specific problems? Are you trying to *quantify* your current culture? What do you expect people to do with the results? What does management want to do with the results?

Is your 360-degree survey performance-based?

Will raters be able to observe the behaviors and practices in the participant they are evaluating? Are the behaviors clearly understood by all raters? Do the behaviors identify performance-related issues that arise when people actually interact with others? Do the behaviors and practices include what people actually do? Have you included attitudinal- or personality-based items in your survey? Will your existing training help participants improve? Can participants change their behaviors either through guided experiences or training or coaching, for example?

Is it comprehensive and relevant?

An effective instrument reflects what your organization sees as critical core competencies and what the raters—internal or external—will take the time to respond to. Who selected the competencies or themes for your survey? Why did you choose these and not others? Are these competencies applicable to all employees being assessed? Or are they intended for a particular level of management, a particular function?

If you have the time and patience, conduct pre-instrument interviews, focus groups, and departmental or functional meetings to identify core issues. Ask yourself:

- Will the survey cover the primary issues you want to measure?
- Will the survey focus on what the author (internal or external)

believes is important? And does that match your requirements (at least for the short term)?
- Who has provided input for what to measure and why?
- How relevant is their input?
- What are their qualifications?
- Who has the expertise in your organization to develop your survey?
- What management principles or research will you use to create your survey?
- How many competencies will you include?
- How many items will you include as a minimum for each competency? (I suggest five items per competency-theme as a minimum.)
- How many items in total will you have, including demographics and open-ended comments (if applicable)? Include those items and competencies that are job-relevant and critical, not just nice to know or nice to have. Decide if you want to include both quantitative and qualitative responses.
- What response scale(s) will you use to collect quantitative feedback?
- Do you want to use a single- or dual-response scale?
- What behavioral anchors will you use for your response scale(s)?
- What types of free-text or open-ended comments do you want to include and why?
- What format will you use—paper or electronic, or a combination of both?
- If you use paper, how and who will enter the data—by hand, scanning, etc.?
- If you include qualitative comments (e.g., open-ended comments), will you edit any responses? Who will you entrust to do this for you?
- If you use the Internet, does each rater (internal and external) have an e-mail address and ready access to the Internet?

Issues for Development

- Are the items understandable? Are the items written in everyday terms? Are the items short and to the point? Do items include two or more practices? Are the items negatively worded or "reverse" items?

- Did you write clear and concise instructions for raters so they can complete your survey with the least amount of confusion possible?
- Did you include the contact information for your liaison or administrator who can respond to any questions or concerns raters may have?
- Have you written a cover letter or initial e-mail notification message? What you say and how you say it can influence whether raters take the time and initiative to complete your instrument or toss it.

There are other issues to consider:

- Write at least one follow-up reminder message for any outstanding raters. This should ensure a higher rate of return.
- Identify the competencies; define each competency (optional); write observable items based on your definition (your Web-based system should include templates to help you design your questionnaire, instructions, cover letters, follow-up reminders).
- Make it easy for people to complete your survey. If you use paper forms, package all materials including the return envelope together. Always include postage when you want feedback from your external customers (metered postage). Include postage for employees as well or let them know that they can use the company mail department to return their survey to either the external vendor or an internal person.
- Give your competencies simple and easily recognizable labels, such as "Delegation," "Problem Solving," "Coaching," "Integrity." Avoid jargon and any whiz-bang labels you found in a book or heard from a speaker. No one else will understand them.
- Use simple and direct language when you write your survey items (questions).
- If you can see it, you can measure it. Write about observable behavioral indicators and practices.
- Proof your efforts within the team before you show it to anyone outside the team. Check for typos, grammatical errors, unclear instructions, etc.
- Then proof everything again.

Issues for Revisions

- Critique any and all suggestions for change. Discuss those changes with your team.
- Revise your instrument, as necessary, based on what you learned from the pilot (and any other comments or sudden insights).
- Finalize your instrument and ready it for deployment.

Issues for Deployment

- Consider writing a pre-survey notification letter/memo/ e-mail alerting your employees or customers that your instrument will be sent to them within the next (XX) days. This may contribute to their trust. It may prepare them better. It may build expectations. It may reduce the possibility raters will delete or discard your survey when it arrives (then claim, of course, that they did not receive it).
- Consider describing the purpose of the instrument.
- Consider why direct reports should provide feedback to their immediate bosses or why customers should provide feedback to their salesperson.
- Consider including the name-signature of a key (and credible) person who could lend credibility to the process when you ask external customers for their feedback.
- Identify why this particular group of people will be assessed first.
- Identify benefits to the person or organization being evaluated.
- Identify benefits to the rater for taking the time to complete the survey.
- Explain how you intend to use the results and who will see the results.
- Make certain you emphasize the confidentiality and anonymity of responses (and keep the data confidential and anonymous).

Issues for Administration

- Who will administer the process? Who will follow up with any outstanding raters? How much time will it take to administer the process? Does this person have the time? What other tasks does (s)he have to do on a daily basis? Does IT have to become involved? Can a non-technical person administer the entire process for you? Do you trust administrators to have access to the data?

- Consider selecting at least two people to act as administrators. These are the folks who have the ID and password to the system. They can access any and all data for anyone.
- Administrators do not necessarily create the surveys. Others can do that. You can do that, then have the administrators enter your competencies and items and rating scales onto the Web-based system for you.
- Administrators have learned how to use the Web-based software. Folks who have not learned it should not be allowed to access it. They will mess it up! Even if they are key decision makers, they have no business with the software. The administrators can print out whatever the decision maker needs so they can review the content, make their eleventh hour changes, and return those changes to the administrator.
- Administrators should encourage employees and customers to respond quickly, as in within seventy-two hours. Most raters will not, of course. However, if you give people three weeks to complete the survey, many will tend to procrastinate until that time then decide to complete it (or whine about why they did not have enough time). The quicker the urgency to respond, the higher the return rate, the fewer the follow-up reminders, the less hassle and administrative morass. I recommend sooner rather than later, and certainly a one-week window is sufficient for anyone who has only one survey to complete.
- Allow more time for those who may have three to six assessments to complete. For example, identify any personnel (e.g., the immediate boss) who have to complete assessments on each of their direct reports. How much extra time to allow? My suggestion is that raters complete one but not more than two assessments per day. Completing multiple assessments in the same day may cause brain atrophy, ennui, and not provide the participant with as relevant feedback as (s)he might need and expect. After one or two assessments the person doing the rating tends to enter automatic responses in an effort to complete the remaining assessments as quickly as possible.

Issues for Delivering the Results

There are a wide variety of reporting formats to consider. Some vendors provide cursory reports while others provide more comprehensive formats. Some reports are dummied down so people (including consultants) do not have to think very much about their influence and effectiveness with others, while other reports require at least a four-year college degree. As a starting point, consider the following to get you thinking.

- Will participants understand the results? What will the data look like? Will you include text and graphic reports? Will you use one of those snappy spreadsheet formats with columns and rows of numbers? Will the data summarize strengths and developmental needs? Will you include a detailed item analysis of each item on your survey? Will you organize open-ended comments by certain themes or categories?
- How will rater feedback be presented? Will the data be reported by each respective rater group, e.g., "Self," "Boss," "Direct Reports," "Peers," "Customer Group A," and "Customer Group B?" Or will the data be lumped together and reported according to "Self" and "Others?" If participants request feedback from two bosses, will the data be reported by each boss (e.g., Boss A and Boss B), or combined into one boss group?
- When will they see their results? Once your survey is deployed, when can participants expect to view the results? How will they interpret their results? Will you include a trained internal or external person to help? Will you leave it up to each participant to interpret their own results? If you include a trained facilitator, will this be in a private one-on-one session, or in a workshop? What materials will you provide to help participants understand their results?
- What will you require participants to do with their feedback results? Nothing? Will participants be required to follow up with someone and share those results? If so, with whom and when? What if participants do nothing with their feedback, except perhaps to toss it? What are the consequences of their sharing their results and of implementing self-directed action plans? What are the consequences to the department or organization if people do something or do nothing?

Issues for Evaluating the Process

- How did it go? What would you do differently the next time? Would you add, modify, or delete any competencies? Items? Instructions?
- How did participants respond to their data? Did they learn anything new about themselves? How many took the initiative to share their feedback with others (e.g., their immediate bosses and direct reports)?
- Were the immediate managers willing to take the time to meet with the participants? Were they effective coaches and mentors?
- Did personnel provide resources to participants so they could resolve any developmental needs? That is, are there in-house training programs available to participants?
- Will the organization fund registration fees for participants who want to take external programs?
- Where does your process (and instrument) go from here? Was this a one-time event?

Personal Accountability for Organizational Success

Some organizations are much more successful doing 360-degree assessments than are others. There are multiple reasons why this occurs. It could be the assessment itself, it could be the vendor, it could be the internal support by key decisions makers within the organization. It could be the extent to which participants and their respective raters take the process of giving and receiving feedback seriously. It could be something about the participants' willingness to change. It could be about reinforcement, or it could be about the consequences of their actions as it affects the people they interact with. Regardless, successful client applications share some common attributes. Here are some of those attributes:

When you hold people accountable for the consequences of their behavior, you reinforce positive behavior-change.

The Role of Your Assessment:

- The 360-degree assessment must be performance-based. It should measure what people do on the job. It should not measure attitudes or style or preferences or test knowledge.
- Consider measuring current behavior compared to expectations: what do raters see a person doing compared to what they expect of that person?
- Include a pre-post assessment component. The POST-assessment should be conducted not earlier than six months from the PRE-assessment, nor longer than thirteen months from the PRE-assessment.

The Role of Participants: They . . .

- Share their feedback with others, especially with their immediate boss.
- Create self-directed action plans with accountability.
- Complete any needed training and development programs.
- Complete a post-assessment with the same feedback survey within a thirteen-month time frame.
- Take responsibility for their behaviors on the job.
- Take a more proactive role in their development.
- Willingly choose to modify their behaviors and expend the effort to do so.
- Share their feedback results with their immediate managers and/or HR within two weeks to identify ways to build on their strengths and to resolve any developmental needs.
- Are accountable for their actions and are willing to implement self-directed action plans based on the feedback results.
- Meet with their immediate bosses on a monthly basis to discuss any progress and to suggest additional ways the participant can improve.

The Role of Bosses: They . . .

- Become a mentor to the participant.
- Provide on-going and frequent coaching.
- Provide input for action plans and training initiatives when necessary.

- Take responsibility for following up with participants.
- Use the feedback for developmental purposes.
- Do not use the feedback to criticize, blame, punish, or otherwise discipline the participant.
- Become positive role models to their employees by being the first (or one of the first) to be assessed by the 360-degree process, then sharing the results with their direct reports.
- Know that not all developmental efforts require training. Understand that many times a person can become more effective through coaching and through a mentor, who is in the same company. The boss can provide this function.
- Are able and willing to coach and reinforce the participants' efforts to change. If not, then HR or an external coach should provide this support.

The Role of Human Resources: HR . . .

- Provides training and other initiatives that support the development of participants.
- Integrates the 360-degree feedback process with other initiatives, such as performance appraisal and career development.
- Assesses upper managerial levels first, then cascades the 360-degree process down the organizational chart.
- Designs programs that include the behaviors from the assessment. Any training and development efforts should align with the feedback assessment itself. That is, if the survey measures delegating then any training program on delegation should include what is measured in the assessment.
- Positions the 360-degree process as an ongoing method for helping employees become more effective. It should not be seen as a fad or a one-off event.
- Does more than talk about feedback.

The primary reasons for failure of a 360-degree process are the inability or unwillingness of the organization to support the participants' efforts to change and to become more effective. Some organizations assume that the feedback alone will cause the participant to improve. That is not always true. The organization has to be willing to have some training programs in place, they have to be willing to go outside the organization

The question for both the boss and the participant is, "How will we hold each other accountable for [the participant's] success?"

and work with external consultants where needed, and they have to make an effort to have these programs and services in place. If these are available to the participant, almost always the participant will improve. Now, if the participant chooses not to take advantage of these programs and services offered by the organization, then it is not the fault of the 360-degree assessment or HR. It is the fault of the participant for not wanting to improve. That is, if the participant is unwilling to improve and change his/her behavior, then no 360-degree assessment and no training or no coaching will help. In short, the organization has an obligation to help their employees reach their potential, to help them become more effective. The participant has an obligation to create action plans that build on their strengths and resolve areas for development.

The Role of Group Profiles:

Successful organizations also use group profiles, aggregated data by a range of demographics, to make needed changes in the organization. The data from these profiles helps:

- Identify training and development needs for specific functions, locations, and other demographics within the organization.
- Trainers-developers modify training and development programs based on the feedback results to create needs driven training initiatives.
- Verify core competencies that apply to all employees or competencies that are more relevant for specific functions.
- Sales organizations create a more competitive edge.

Organizational Integration of 360: Connections

This book is about creating 360-degree feedback assessments — from design to delivery. You develop an assessment for some purpose, some goal, or some application. All too often the assessment is not aligned with any specific program or process within the organization. Employees may not always see the connection between a 360-degree feedback process and the organization's training and development programs. This section focuses on how you can integrate performance-based 360-degree assessments into your existing (or future) training and development programs.

You can develop any assessment as a stand-alone event without connecting it to any other initiative or program or process within your organization. You can also integrate your assessment with one or more programs and make the connection between those programs and the participants on a participant-by-participant basis, or by aggregating the results from multiple participants from a specific function or location or any other demographic. When you make such connections between your assessment and a training and development program, you reinforce why your organization has the assessment and a particular training program. You create value for both the assessment and the program. Your employees understand the relationship and the value for continuous learning and development.

All too often training programs about leadership or management development or communication skills have little connection between a career development track or succession planning process or a team-building initiative. The feedback results from a 360-degree assessment that measures leadership competencies can typically be applied to a training program on leadership development, a dual-career development track, your succession planning process, or as part of your performance management process for managerial personnel. The feedback results also help clarify expectations, up front, between the employee and a new favorite boss.

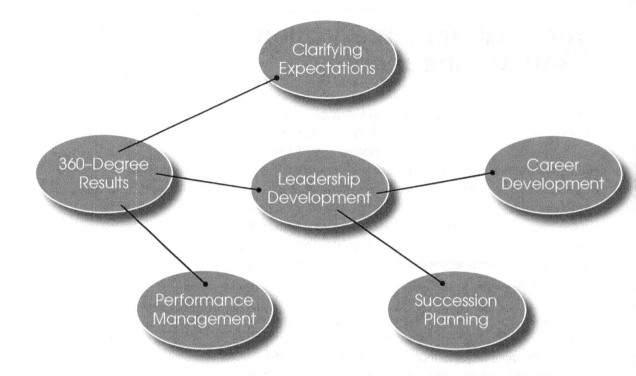

Integrate your performance-based 360-degree assessments with your training and development programs.

Consider these three primary applications as a starting point to connect your 360-degree assessment to other initiatives within your organization:

A. Needs-Driven Training and Development
B. Career Development
C. Clarifying Expectations

A. Needs-Driven Training and Development

Training Needs Analyses: Use the 360-degree results to *create* needs-driven training programs. Aggregate the data from multiple participants and from different functions to identify the collective strengths and weaknesses for a particular target population and/or for all of the employees who have completed the same 360-degree assessment. If you develop your training programs internally, have your developers focus on those same developmental needs to create more relevant training programs. Or, contact your favorite vendor and have them include those areas in the program to meet your key developmental needs. You create greater value for your employees and greater credibility for yourself and the HR function by "personalizing" the training to what employees need based upon the feedback. Can you include other content areas in the program? Of course, but the primary focus connects the feedback results with the content of the program and the target population.

Modify Existing Programs: Again, use the 360-degree feedback results to identify those areas in your *existing* training programs that you may need to modify. Use the feedback results to drive what you need to modify in order to keep your programs as relevant as possible. When you administer the feedback process continuously over time, you can identify training trends that will help you expand upon those content areas (competency areas) that employees are weakest in, and you will shorten the in-session training time spent on those content areas that are consistently identified as strengths.

Create Training Tracks: Use the feedback results to *gate* employees into those training and development initiatives they need to help them develop and reach their potential. This proactive approach will save you money and increase the motivational level of those who attend. You could organize your training programs to focus on task and relationship competencies. The employee can register for programs they need rather than attend programs that would be "nice" for them to have or that they have to attend to fulfill some arbitrary requirement that says employees need a certain amount of training hours to maintain their professionalism or whatever. Stop focusing on numbers of training hours completed. If you want employees to perform more effectively or be more professional or whatever, use their feedback to drive their development.

Integrate Training with Feedback: You can make your one-day or multi-day training programs more relevant to employees by connecting the program directly to a performance-based 360-degree assessment. As I mentioned earlier in this book, create and integrate a 360-degree assessment that aligns with a particular training program. Employees review their feedback results for each competency area immediately prior to the trainer-facilitator covering each area during the program. You create greater value when employees understand why the program includes the content that it does. The program connects to the competencies measured by the 360-degree assessment and vice versa. If one of your shorter training programs focuses on a single competency area such as delegating to others, for example, create a mini-360 assessment that measures the key learning points from your delegation program. The connection between a shorter 360 assessment and a more content-focused training program allows employees to target their developmental efforts, without having to sit through content areas they do not need to develop because those are not areas of weakness for them.

Integrate Training with Pre-Post Feedback: You can measure the progress people are making towards their self-directed action plans when you integrate pre-post assessments in your training and development initiatives. Employees create action plans and complete any needed training and development based on their pre-assessment. Give them time to apply what they have learned, then conduct a post-assessment to measure the extent to which they have applied what they have learned effectively. If there are areas they still need to improve upon, gate them into a program that focuses on the content area(s) they need, such as "Delegating to Others," to name one example.

Blended Learning: You can increase the effectiveness of your training and development process by connecting your traditional training programs with Web-based developmental resources and your 360-degree assessment process. Employees can use their feedback results to identify which Web-based programs and resources to access. A blended learning approach accommodates the different ways people prefer to learn, e.g., self-instructional and self-paced or live, instructor-led group interactions. Continue to use your traditional training programs for the "heart and soul" of the content you want to cover and the Web-based sources as a remedial program. Or, use the Web sources as the foundation for the content and your (modified) instructor-led training program for the application of what employees learned online. If your organization has an online corporate university, create a matrix or developmental guide for participants by identifying which programs they can take advantage of and in which medium—self-instructional, Web-based, or instructor-led workshop sessions.

Outdoor Learning: You can dramatically increase the value of your outdoor experiential learning program by aligning it with a performance-based 360-degree assessment. Establishing this connection will help participants understand the consequences of their behavior from the people who gave them their feedback and with those who they are now "role playing" with in each outdoor learning exercise. You can create the 360-degree assessment first, then develop the outdoor learning exercises to complement the assessment — or if you already have the outdoor learning program, create the assessment that complements the outcomes for the program. You help participants identify the consequences of their on-the-job-behavior with their behavior during the outdoor exercises.

For example, does your organization send people into the wilderness to bungee-jump off teeny-tiny-feet-itching-heart-pounding-platforms way up high in the air and have them cross bodies of mucky-yucky water using whatever materials they find in the hopes that they can cross from one side of the pond to the other before sinking? Do you have them fall backwards into the waiting outstretched arms of their comrades in the heart-throbbing hope that the person will be caught before someone says OOOPS? What is the purpose of the outdoor learning program? What is the purpose of each exercise? Why, for example, do you have people bungee-jumping or fording a body of water? If one purpose is to develop better inter- or intra-departmental cooperation, how effectively do the employees in the outdoor program do this now, before they come to the program, and how do you know? A performance-based 360-degree assessment can identify their inter/intra-departmental cooperative strengths and weaknesses before they begin the outdoor program.

Collect the feedback from the participant's favorite boss, direct reports, and peers as you would normally, and compile the 360-degree feedback prior to the experiential learning event. Create both individual and group profiles to identify strengths and weaknesses. Implement the outdoor learning program as you would normally do it: conduct the exercises; observe how participants resolve problems and make decisions and how they communicate and collaborate with one another. Observers debrief the exercise based upon what each participant did and how they performed, and so on. Then have participants review

> **Compare "work behavior" with "play behavior."**

their 360 feedback results for each of those competencies included in a particular exercise or group of exercises, e.g., problem solving and decision making and communication, and so on. Does their 360 feedback mirror the feedback from the outdoor learning observers? Are there differences? What are the consequences to the participant for behaving differently?

Style-Type Surveys: You can help employees understand the consequences for what and how they *prefer* to do their work and interact with others with how they *actually perform* their work and conduct their interactions by administering a style-type and a performance-based 360 assessment. Style-type surveys identify one's preference for working with others, for making decisions, for organizing tasks and prioritizing work, and so on. The employee may prefer to make decisions alone or they may prefer to lead others or prefer to control a discussion. A 360 assessment identifies *how effectively* the employee does what (s)he prefers to do. You cannot know this from a style-type assessment, but you can with a 360-degree assessment. People should be able to understand the extent to which their preferences align with their on-the-job effectiveness. Of course, you may not care to focus on effectiveness, but rather style. Nonetheless, connecting the two can dramatically help people build on their strengths and minimize their weaknesses.

Style-type surveys identify one's preferences. Performance-based 360 assessments can identify how effectively the person does what (s)he prefers to do.

B. Career Development

Performance Appraisals: Linking a performance appraisal process with 360-degree feedback is a sensitive issue for some people, yet connecting the two will provide much greater value and serve as a more effective developmental process for employees. Connecting the two can serve as a catalyst for implementing needed behavior change and can also reinforce action planning.

Traditionally, the immediate boss has been the primary appraiser of the employee's performance. Some organizations allow the employee to appraise him/herself, and other organizations include upward feedback from the direct reports. You can replace your boss only or boss-employee performance appraisal with a 360-degree assessment or complement your performance appraisal format with a 360 assessment. The critical point here is to align them both by including the performance related themes-competencies from your performance appraisal process in your 360-degree assessment. If your performance appraisal includes themes such as "Verbal and Written Communication," "Problem Solving and Decision Making," "Delegating," " Working with Others," and so on, then include behaviorally written questions in your 360 assessment for these same themes-competencies.

Performance Management: Some folks turn green about the gills when they believe feedback and appraisals will immediately be tied to compensation. That is a misuse of the 360-degree process. You can easily connect the feedback process with compensation and keep folks comfy when you separate the feedback from compensation. Performance management is an extension of your appraisal process. And as I have mentioned, the 360-degree assessment can provide value-added benefits to your "appraisal-evaluation" process.

If you have a boss-employee performance appraisal and conduct it as an annual or semi-annual event, administer the appraisal and the 360 assessment at about the same time. Use the feedback from both appraisals as baseline data. The employee can develop action plans based on the results and suggestions from the boss. Re-administer the 360-degree assessment six to eleven months later and compare the results and, depending on those results, decide what compensation the employee has earned based upon multiple appraisals and multiple raters over an agreed-to time period.

Dual-Career Tracks: Employees will benefit and contribute more to the organization when they are in an area or function that utilizes their strengths. Does your 360 assessment include both task and relationship competencies? If not create (or purchase) one. The feedback results should identify whether or not the participant is highly effective in both areas or highly effective in one area. Depending on the results and the career aspirations of the participant, (s)he can decide to remain and advance in, say research and development, because (s)he is highly effective in all (or almost all) of the task competencies. Conversely, someone may be highly effective in their relationship competencies and would welcome the opportunity to move out of research and into the fun-filled world of managing people. You can easily integrate the 360-degree (include both a pre- and post-assessment) and performance appraisal results with your existing dual-career development track. If you do not have such a developmental track, have the folks in personnel create the parameters for such a program, and include those critical competencies employees need to succeed in each specific job or those functions that require more task strengths than people strengths and vice versa.

Training and Promotions: There are many benefits for using a 360-degree assessment to identify your high potentials and developing them before you promote them. Often organizations promote folks before they have received training, especially people-oriented training. The person may know what to do in the new position but may lack the people skills needed to create a motivated and productive team. You can administer a pre- and post-assessment process to confirm the person's potential. Provide the employee with any needed training and development they need *before* you actually promote them, i.e., between the pre- and post-assessment. Build upon the person's competency *before* they have the opportunity to fail.

Succession Planning: Use your 360 assessment(s) to build your bench-strength throughout the organization. Develop a performance-based 360-degree assessment based upon the competencies a person needs to succeed in key positions. Multiple performance appraisals and 360 results will provide a succession planning committee with a more complete snapshot of the candidate's performance and effectiveness. Pre- and post-assessments can confirm strengths and track the candidate's progress towards resolving any identified weaknesses.

Assessment Centers: You can introduce more "reality" in your assessment center program when you integrate a 360-degree assessment. As I mentioned in the outdoor learning application, participants should be able to compare their on-the-job effectiveness with their behavior in the assessment center. Develop a 360 assessment based on the exercises and competencies included in your assessment center program. One outcome of an assessment center is to identify someone's potential for success in the same job or function or in a different job or function. Assessment centers attempt to get at this "potential success" through exercises and role playing. Some folks are very good at playing the desired role during those exercises and, as a result, may "fool" the observers. Performance-based 360 assessments can identify actual success and effectiveness. The feedback participants receive is based upon what raters have observed the participant doing on the job, handling real day-to-day situations and problems. Administer the 360 process prior to the assessment center session. Facilitators can decide when to review the 360 results with participants, though it is often better to do this after each exercise has been completed and/or when the facilitators debrief participants about how they have fared at various segments within the assessment center program.

Coaches and Mentors: You cannot coach or mentor someone unless you know what the critical issues are for that person. Use the 360-degree results to identify the types of developmental activities the coach or mentor needs to consider when working with the participant. This will make each coaching or mentoring session specific to the participant based on what the data says they need, not what the participant says they need. It will help the coach or mentor keep the participant on task and on a feedback-driven agenda.

Identifying Coaches and Mentors: You can hire external coaches and mentors to help your people develop, or you can use the 360-degree feedback results to identify people within your organization who could fulfill those roles for you. This will save you money and allow you to tap into the high performers within your organization, those who speak the same "language" and know the politics of the organization from "square one." You already "paid" for the 360 assessment, so use that same data to identify who are the most effective people in a particular competency or who are effective in all of the task and/or relationship competencies. The key is to identify someone who is highly effective in a competency, that is, someone who has no gaps or developmental needs in that area. If there are ten questions that measure a competency, the person should be highly effective in all ten behaviors. This person could be a coach for that specific competency. Ideally, that same person would be highly effective in related competencies, e.g., task or relationship, and would be willing to be the coach or mentor in those areas as well.

C. Clarifying Expectations

The New Boss and You: Use the 360-degree feedback results to help create a better dialog between the boss and his/her direct reports. What if *you* learned that you would be reporting to a new boss? What does (s)he expect from you? What new and different style will you need to contend with? What new and exciting performance surprises await you? What will it take for you to break in this new person so the two of you can work more effectively with one another? Have you completed a 360-degree assessment? If so, share your results with the new boss. You can easily identify your strengths and any areas for development, and indicate how you and your previous boss worked together. Share this with your new favorite boss. You need to know if what you were doing yesterday will be effective today with the new boss. Use your 360-degree feedback results to clarify those expectations, up front, before you receive your first performance appraisal and before, perhaps, you find a sudden urge to update your résumé.

The New Employee and You: Apply the "new boss and you" recommendation to a newly hired employee. Help your new hires perform more effectively and more quickly. Hire the best performing employees you can. Provide them with whatever coaching and training and mentoring you can during their first three months on the job. Then administer a 360-degree assessment that aligns with their position, e.g., individual contributor, first line supervisor, manager. Use the results as baseline data. Provide opportunities for the employee to improve and develop and include a coach (internal or external) if necessary. Administer a post-assessment within the year, but not earlier than six months from the pre-assessment, to coincide with your regular performance appraisal. You need to provide sufficient time for the employee to learn and apply any new ideas designed to resolve identified weaknesses. Then compare the results. Your goal here is to clarify up front what is expected of the employee, provide them with opportunities to build on strengths, and resolve any identified weakness early in their career. When you are proactive and clarify performance expectations up front, employees understand what they need to do to succeed and what the consequences are if they do not meet expectations.

Proactive Examples: Beyond Woo-Woo

Facilitator's Ice-Breaker

Anyone who has ever facilitated a training or feedback session opens the program with some kind of ice-breaker to make folks feel as comfy as possible before getting to the heart of the program. The facilitator may use multiple ice-breakers depending on their style and their audience. What works for one facilitator may not necessarily work for another. Here is one exercise to consider for an ice-breaker.

At the start of every feedback workshop, I ask participants two questions. "How do you think you will respond if the feedback you are about to receive is much more positive (however you define positive) than you had ever dreamed was possible?" Participants respond. I write the responses on a flip chart. That works for me. The comments range anywhere from "gee-golly" to "aww-shucks" to "that couldn't happen to me." They range from guarded exuberance to excessive modesty. Done. Then I ask the second question to only those who responded to my first question: "How do you think you will respond if the feedback you are about to receive is much more negative (however you define negative) than you had anticipated?" Initially, the comments are almost always textbook. Participants say they will see that feedback as developmental, as a challenge, as a beacon of light that has identified some opportunities, as a way to grow and as an ongoing process to be the best they can be, and so on. I write these on the flip chart as well. I plaster my flips on the wall for all to see. And I wait. Very soon someone will drop the cutesy textbook responses and say they would not be happy campers at all if they received "negative feedback." They would not like the data. They would question the heritage (or lack thereof) of the airheads who gave them that feedback. They would not look very kindly on those village idiots, nor their feedback. Other participants express their outright anger and disappointment. Bless their hearts! These types of non-textbook responses legitimize the feelings of others—positive and negative. Participants feel more comfy sharing their feedback with others in the workshop. There is support in this environment. They discuss their action plans. They talk about next steps. They talk about applying their results. That is the reaction I tend to look for. That is my ice-breaker for a 360-degree feedback workshop.

Participant's Ice-Breaker

There are many ice-breakers you can use to open your feedback sessions. Yet, there are times when one or more participants can make the other participants feel at ease and receptive to what the facilitator has planned for the session. Here is one example that I continue to appreciate even to this day.

We were the first organization to introduce 360-degree feedback in South East Asia in 1992. Initially, we conducted public sessions where only one or two participants from an organization attended. Some sessions included competitors; some participants were evaluating the process for themselves; some for their organization; and others out of general curiosity. One key vice president from a large bank helped us succeed in SE Asia, perhaps even more than our marketing efforts and that of the alliances we created with local consultants. He was one of sixteen participants in a full-day workshop we conducted in this country. In the morning we discussed each reporting format, how to interpret it, and how to apply the results through self-directed action plans. Our True Gap Analysis™ process was a new concept at that time and it turned out to be quite intriguing to them. As we explored our unique concept, this vice president suddenly got up and shared his feedback with two of his peers from two different companies. He was marveling at the feedback he received from his boss and was wondering out loud if others had similar feedback. They did. One shared her wonderment at the feedback she received from her direct reports. Well, there were many giggles to be sure. Yet what he did for the rest of the group was fantastic. His sharing of his feedback encouraged almost everyone else in the room to do the same. Suddenly, their feedback became everyone else's feedback. The interchange was great. While I responded to their questions, they responded to each other's feedback, and though they were from different organizations they seemed quite willing to help each other understand their results and decide on strategies to share those results with others once they returned to work. The culture in many Asian countries (at least in the early '90s) sees feedback not necessarily as developmental but as criticism. When you received feedback, you probably were doing something wrong. There was a need to save face. (Of course, people in the West have the same need; we don't like being embarrassed or shamed either.) These were brave souls to be the first to go through the process and implement action plans. Yet, thanks to this VP and his reputation, people understood the value of the process, the value of understanding the consequences of their behavior, and how different rater groups can have different expectations of the same participant.

Self-Directed Action Planning: Applying the Results

The third example is a letter we received from a recent participant to our process. She was writing this to her team, letting them know what she learned and what she intended to do with the feedback results. The words are hers, though I have edited references to people and her organization. She went through her data in a one-on-one session with one of our CCi Consultants, and here is what she wrote as a result of that interaction:

Last Friday, I had the pleasure of spending four hours with [the CCi Consultant], reviewing and discussing my personal results as it relates to the 360-degree coaching guide process. I can assure the group that this was a very educational, beneficial, and time-well-spent personal development process — not to mention enjoyable. By the end of the first half of this year, the entire management team [a region within the USA] will be afforded the opportunity to participate in this personal development process. The primary purpose why the company is investing the time, energy, and money into this program is to make all of us more effective managers and better [professionals]. In addition, another benefit of this process, which from my perspective is the most important one, is to make us more effective and well-rounded people as it relates to our business, family, and personal lives. Based on the valuable input from my boss, three of my

You make a difference not with a big title, but with a little caring.

colleagues and three of my direct reports, the coaching guide survey has indicated a number of areas I need to improve my management style and skills in.

I need to do more of the following with [this particular rater group]:

Communication
Demonstrate that you have been heard and understood
Appear to be more approachable and easier to talk with
Allow you to finish what you have to say

Coaching
Maintain a system or procedure to evaluate your performance
Provide feedback when your work does not meet my personal expectations
Treat mistakes as a learning experience

Delegation
Assignments and responsibilities to match your individual capabilities
Identify up front how your performance will be measured
Let you know what is expected of you before beginning a task

Additional Things I Will Do to Become More Effective
Trust my management team more
Allow you to make and learn from your decisions
Not criticize as much
Learn to slow down and not go at such a fast pace so I can learn to catch and accept your thought process and ideas before responding
Learn to listen better, to be more patient
Demonstrate a greater degree of mentoring and allow my management team to use their initiatives and thought process in a more open manner

Things That I Should Stop Doing to Become More Effective
Learn to stop taking the opposing point of view at times and saying to the management team, "You did it this way — why couldn't you have done it that way?"
Less micromanagement
Learn to be a little more aggressive
With the intention of making sure that I stay the course, hit the target. and above all achieve success, I am going to ask

that [my immediate manager] serve as my consigliore and keep me apprised on how I am doing in all of these areas of needed improvement based on your feedback to him. Therefore, beginning next Friday and then every other Friday thereafter, would you please call me at your convenience and apprise from your perspective and that of your peers after discussion with them as required, to let me know if I, as the student, am making progress in developing into a more effective manager and leader. Secondly, at our future quarterly management meetings, I am going to allocate an hour or more so that we can personally discuss, face-to-face, the progress that is being made by me in these areas of development, in addition, so we can discuss openly ways that I can continue to improve my management style and skills with the goal and objective of striving to be the best of the best.

In closing I thank those who participated in the 360-degree coaching guide process for their honest, frank, and direct comments. I personally look forward to working with the team to achieve our mutual goals and objectives in this area.

I have been actively involved in the "360-degree movement" since 1976. Some days are more fun than other days. Some days I meet people who are willing and sincere about working more effectively with others. Some days I meet people who are more concerned about how they can contribute to the organization, rather than worrying about the size of their office. Thank you!

Planning for Behavior Change: The Able and Willing

Rationalization is the

key to mental health.

I wrote this book to make you more aware of the core components needed to create a more effective performance-based 360-degree assessment. My hope is that you apply these proven techniques and create more effective assessments for your organization and for your clients, internal or external. The content of this book represents the easy part. You can learn and apply any of the ideas in this book. You are the catalyst for creating more effective 360-degree assessments.

Yet, the issue is not whether you can do it, but rather, to what extent are you willing to do it? Understanding it is the easy part. Doing it is the hard part.

Participants are similar. You can design a performance-based 360-degree assessment, develop and deploy it, and deliver the results in either a one-on-one or group feedback session. What happens when participants receive their results? All participants should be able to understand your reporting formats and, as a result, identify their strengths to build upon and weaknesses to resolve. There is nothing terribly cerebral about analyzing one's data. Like you, they are able to do the easy part. And, like you, to what extent are they willing to do things differently as a result of the feedback they just received?

Your job may be to build an assessment and provide a means for delivering the results to participants. Perhaps others within your organization will be responsible for helping participants move forward and create self-directed action plans based on the feedback results. Perhaps others will provide the training or the coaching or the mentoring or the follow-up to reinforce the behaviors each participant has identified as a goal for a specific time line.

The best 360-degree assessment, the best 360-degree process is irrelevant unless and until participants apply what they have learned from their feedback.

Participants have the ability to understand their feedback results. Typically, they will commit to creating action plans when they buy into their results, when they are emotionally ready to do so. Participants can go through the physical motions of writing an action plan, yet until their emotions (and egos) allow them to move forward, not much of their behavior will change in the direction recommended by the feedback. Action plans should be feedback-driven. Action plans need to come from one's head and heart and not just from one's hand.

Again, the issue is not whether the participant can do it, but rather, to what extent is the participant willing to do it? Understanding it is the easy part. Doing it is the hard part.

The best 360-degree assessment, the best 360-degree process is irrelevent unless and until the participants apply what they have learned from their feeback.

CCi Surveys International

CCi Surveys International can provide you with the most comprehensive suite of 360-degree feedback surveys. We can modify any of our assessments to meet your needs.

 We invite you to visit our Web site: **www.ccisurveys.com**.

Data Privacy Statement

In October, 1998, the European Union (EU) adopted the Directive on Data Protection which sets forth strict rules for companies handling personal data about EU citizens. This restriction includes companies in the United States because of a small provision which prevents the transfer of data to any country which does not have "an adequate level of privacy." CCi Surveys International is in compliance with both the European Union Privacy Directive on Data Protection and the USA International Safe Harbor Privacy Principles administered by the FTC. Specifically, CCi Surveys International ...

Notifies corporate decision makers, employees, and consumers about how information collected about them will be used;

Uses data for its intended purpose;

Does not knowingly transfer data on employees and consumers to countries with inadequate privacy protection laws;

Allows employees and consumers the right to access data collected about them;

Allows employees and consumers the right to have inaccurate data rectified;

Allows employees and consumers the right to know the origin of data about them (if this information is available);

Allows employees and consumers the right of recourse in the event of unlawful processing of data about them;

Allows employees and consumers the right to withhold permission to use their data (e.g., the right to opt out of direct marketing campaigns for free without providing a reason);

Does not process sensitive information about employees or consumers, including information on racial origin, political or religious beliefs, trade union membership, medical data, and sexual life.

Registered Trademarks

The CCi Profiling System®, including the feedback,
action planning, training and development, and follow-up mobias
strip, is a registered trademark of Cipolla Companies, Inc.
and CCi Assessment Group International.

The CCi Profiling System®, including continuous learning for personal
and professional development®, is a registered trademark of Cipolla
Companies, Inc. and CCi Assessment Group International.

. . . . continuous learning for personal
and professional development®

CCi Direct-Connect®, a Web-based software platform,
is a registered trademark of Cipolla Companies, Inc.
and CCi Surveys International.

True-Gap Analysis™ is a registered trademark of
Cipolla Companies, Inc. and CCi Surveys International.

Notes:

Concordance of Selected Topics

Concordance of Selected Topics

Concordance of Selected Topics